Switzerland

Tour boats line the riverbank in the resort of Luzern

AA Publishing

Above: St Bernard dog

Published and distributed in the United Kingdom by
AA Publishing, a trading name of Automobile Association
Developments Limited, whose registered office is
Millstream, Maidenhead Road, Windsor, Berkshire,
SL4 5GD.
Registered number 1878835.

© Automobile Association Developments Limited 2003
Swiss national map and regional maps reproduced by
permission of swisstopo (BA035745)
Town plans reproduced by permission of the Federal
Directorate of Cadastral Surveying (BA035745)
Town plans and Swiss national map © Hallwag
Kümmerly+Frey AG, Ch-3322 Schönbühl-Bern Switzerland

Automobile Association Developments Limited retains the
copyright in the original edition © 2000 and in all
subsequent editions, reprints and amendments
Reprinted 2004.

A CIP catalogue record for this book is available from the
British Library.

The contents of this publication are believed correct at
the time of printing. Nevertheless, the publishers cannot
be held responsible for any errors or omissions or for
changes in the details given in this guide or for the conse-
quences of any reliance on the information it provides. This
does not affect your statutory rights. Assessments of
attractions, hotels, restaurants and other sights are based
upon the author's personal experience and, therefore,
necessarily contain elements of subjective opinion which
may not reflect the publisher's opinion or dictate a reader's
own experience on another occasion.

We have tried to ensure accuracy in this guide, but
things do change and we would be grateful if readers
would advise us of any inaccuracies they may encounter.

*Find out more about
AA Publishing and the
wide range of services
the AA provides by
visiting our web site at
www.theAA.com*

A02006

Colour separation: Keenes Repro
Printed and bound in Italy by Printer Trento srl

Contents

About this Book

This book is divided into 4 sections to cover the most important aspects of your visit to Switzerland.

Practical Matters pages 7–13
A highly visual section containing essential travel information.

An **introduction** to Switzerland pages 14–25
Land of Contrasts
History
Flora & Fauna
The People
Food & Drink
Customs & Folklore
Calender of Events

A **'what to see'** section pages 29–103
Split into seven regions of Switzerland, each with its own brief introduction, and an alphabetical listing of the main places to visit, practical information for attractions and suggested walks and tours in the area.

Note: it may not be possible to access suggested walks and tours during the snowy season. Check with tourist information before setting off.

Special features pages 104–110
Railways & Scenic Journeys
Glaciers
Winter Sports

Where To... pages 113–124
Gives a taster of the best places to eat and stay, and suggestings on where to go for the best shopping and to be entertained.

Prices
Where appropriate, an indication of the cost of an establishment is given by £ signs:
£££ denotes higher prices, ££ denotes average prices, while £ denotes lower charges.

Admission charges
Expensive   = more than CHF13
Moderate   = CHF7–13
Cheap under = CHF7

Essence of Switzerland

Neat gardens and attractive trees frame wooden-built chalets in a typical Swiss valley below sheer hills rising towards snow-clad mountains

Switzerland – from its lush river valleys, rolling hills filled with fruit trees and cows, to its glacial alpine passes, this small nation is truly a natural treasure. Travelling through the country the history, language, culture and cuisine changes from valley to valley. Whatever the season Switzerland is the classic holiday destination and its fast, efficient and frequent public transport system connects even the remotest of places. Explore by foot, bicycle or car to view everything from meadows to stunning peaks, ride high on the cable cars or take a steamboat on one of the pristine lakes. The diversity of landscape is striking, the efficiency and cleanliness refreshing, The visitor benefits from all these aspects with good ski lifts, well-signed walks, pedestrian-only town centres and clean, well-run hotels. Switzerland is a beautiful place and the Swiss will do their best to help you enjoy it to the full.

A pastoral scene of a cow lying peacefully in green pastures

Practical Matters

Above: *Zürich tram*
Right: *the scenic route of the train to Zermatt*

TIME DIFFERENCES

GMT	Switzerland	Germany	USA (NY)	Netherlands	Spain
12 noon	1PM	1PM	7AM	1PM	1PM

WHAT YOU NEED

		UK	Germany	USA	Netherlands	Spain
● Required ○ Suggested ▲ Not required	Some countries require a passport to remain valid for a minimum period (usually at least six months) beyond the date of entry – contact their consulate or embassy or your travel agent for details.					
Passport		●	●	●	●	●
Visa (Regulations can change – check before your journey)		▲	▲	▲	▲	▲
Onward or Return Ticket		▲	▲	▲	▲	▲
Health Inoculations		▲	▲	▲	▲	▲
Health Documentation (► 13, Health)		▲	▲	▲	▲	▲
Travel Insurance		○	○	○	○	○
Driving Licence (national)		●	●	●	●	●
Car Insurance Certificate (if own car)		●	●	●	●	●
Car Registration Document (if own car)		●	●	●	●	●

WHEN TO GO

Zürich

 High season

 Low season

2°C	4°C	8°C	12°C	18°C	21°C	22°C	22°C	18°C	13°C	6°C	2°C
JAN	FEB	MAR	APR	MAY	JUN	JUL	AUG	SEP	OCT	NOV	DEC

Cloud   Sun   Sunshine/Showers

TOURIST OFFICES

In the UK
Switzerland Travel Centre
10th Floor
Swiss Centre
10 Wardour Street
London W1D 6QF
☎ 00800 100 200 30

In the USA
Swiss Centre
608 Fifth Avenue
New York
NY 10020
☎ (212) 757 5944
Fax: (212) 262 6116

POLICE 117

FIRE 118

AMBULANCE 144

AVALANCHE BULLETIN 187

WHEN YOU ARE THERE

ARRIVING

Switzerland has three international airports, at Basel, Genève and Zürich. There are also many domestic airports and a good internal flight system.

Zürich Airport
Distance to city centre

12km

Journey times

🚃 10 minutes

🚌 20 minutes

🚗 15 minutes

Genève Airport
Distance to city centre

5km

Journey times

🚃 6 minutes

🚌 20 minutes

🚗 15 minutes

MONEY

Switzerland's currency is the Swiss franc, issued in 1,000, 200, 100, 50, 20 and 10 franc notes, and 5, 2, 1 and ½ franc coins. There are 100 centimes in a franc, and 20, 10 and 5 centime coins. Traveller's cheques are accepted by most hotels, shops and restaurants in lieu of cash, but the rate of exchange may be less favourable than in banks. Traveller's cheques issued in Swiss francs are most convenient.

Banks can be found in all towns and most villages and handle traveller's cheques, Eurocheques and give cash advances on credit cards.

TIME

 Switzerland is one hour ahead of Greenwich mean time (GMT + 1), but from March to October daylight saving time (GMT + 2) operates, as in the UK.

CUSTOMS

→ **YES**

Visitors from European Countries
Alcohol: up to 15% vol – 2 litres; over 15% vol – 1 litre
Tobacco: 200 cigarettes AND 50 cigars OR 250g pipe tobacco
Perfume: No limit

Visitors from Non-European Countries
Alcohol: up to 15% – vol 2 litres; over 15% vol – 1 litre
Tobacco: 400 cigarettes AND 100 cigars OR 250g pipe tobacco
Perfume: No limit

Visitors must be aged at least 17 to benefit from tobacco and alcohol allowances.

 NO

Drugs, firearms, offensive weapons, obscene material.

UK
(031) 359 7700

Germany
(031) 359 4111

USA
(031) 357 7011

Netherlands
(031) 350 8700

Spain
(031) 352 0412

WHEN YOU ARE THERE

TOURIST OFFICES

Basel
● Aeschenvorstadt 36
CH-4002 Basel
☎ (061) 268 6868
Fax: (061) 268 6870
www.baseltourismus.ch

Bern
● Im Bahnhof
CH-3001 Bern
☎ (031) 328 1212
Fax: (031) 312 1233
www.berntourismus.ch

Genève
● rue du Mont-Blanc 3
CH-1211 Genève
☎ (022) 909 7000
Fax: (022) 909 7075
www.geneva-tourism.ch

Zürich
● Im Hauptbahnhof
CH-8023 Zürich
☎ (01) 215 4000
Fax: (01) 215 4044
www.zurichtourism.ch

Other useful websites:
Switzerland Tourism
www.myswitzerland.com

Information about Switzerland
www.about.ch

The Swiss Embassy in the US
www.swissemb.org

Bernese Oberland
www.berneroberland.com

Valais
www.matterhornstate.com

For skiers
www.skiing.com

NATIONAL HOLIDAYS

J	F	M	A	M	J	J	A	S	O	N	D
1		(2)	(2)	2			1				2

1 Jan	New Year's Day
Mar/Apr	Good Friday
	Easter Monday
May	Ascension Day
	Whit Monday
1 Aug	National Day
25 Dec	Christmas Day
26 Dec	Boxing Day

There are also individual canton holidays, usually 2 Jan, 1 May, Corpus Christi (late May/early June) and Thanksgiving (Sep).

OPENING HOURS

○ Shops   ● Attractions/museums
● Offices   ● Post offices
● Banks   ● Pharmacies

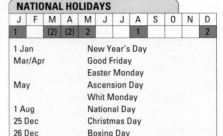

7 AM	8 AM	9 AM	10 AM	12 PM	1 PM	2 PM	3 PM	4 PM	5 PM
	7:30	8:30	9:30	10:30	12:30	1:30	2:30	3:30	4:30

The times given above apply Monday to Friday. On Saturdays shops and pharmacies close at 4PM and post offices at 11AM. Large department stores, supermarkets and shops in tourist areas may open outside the times shown, especially in summer (and winter in winter-sport areas).
Museums are usually open until 9PM on one day each week, and closed on one day a week, usually Monday.

10

DRIVE ON THE RIGHT

TOILETS FREE

PUBLIC TRANSPORT

 Internal Flights Switzerland has a good domestic air service.
Check for flights with Swiss International Airlines (www.swiss.com). You will need to book ahead at the height of the summer and winter seasons. For airport information ring: Basel (061) 325 2511; Bern (031) 960 2111; Genève (022) 717 7111; Zürich (043) 816 2211

 Trains Switzerland has one of the best railway systems in Europe. The system offers a number of savings to visitors. The Swiss Pass allows free travel on services (rail, bus or boat) with validity from four days to one month. The Swiss Flexi Pass allows the visitor to choose three discounted travel days from a 15-day period. The Swiss Card gives a 50 per cent reduction on travel from your airport to your destination and back and reductions on rail, bus and boats. It is valid for one month. There are also regional passes and Family Cards.

 Buses Switzerland has an excellent bus service. Of particular interest to walkers is the Postbus service, which visits even remote alpine villages. These operate to a reliable timetable. Postbuses are yellow and marked by a post horn on a black disc. Their horns play the first notes of Rossini's *William Tell Overture*.

 Ferries The larger lakes have steamer services. There is a Boat Pass available that entitles visitors to a 50 per cent discount for one or two weeks.

CAR RENTAL

 All the major car-hire companies are represented at Swiss airports and railway stations, and have offices in the major towns and cities. Hire cars usually already have a motorway tax (*vignette*).

TAXIS

 Taxis are available at all airports, railway and bus stations, and at key places in large towns and cities.

DRIVING

 Speed limit on motorways: **120kph**
If you are planning to drive on Swiss motorways in your own car you must display a *vignette* (tax sticker) – or risk a fine. It costs Sfr40 and is available at border crossings, post offices and service stations, or in advance from your Swiss Tourist Office.

 Speed limit on main roads: **80kph**
Speed limit on minor roads: **50kph**

 Speed limit in urban areas: **50kph**

 Seat belts are obligatory for drivers and all passengers over the age of 7. Children under 12 years must travel in rear seats.

 Random breath testing is carried out. Limit: 80μg of alcohol in 100ml of breath.

 Petrol stations keep shop hours (though they may be open later in the evening). Even motorway petrol stations close at night. Most petrol stations take credit cards.

 A red warning triangle must be carried and its use is obligatory in case of breakdown or accident. If you break down, the Touring Club of Switzerland (TCS) (022) 417 2727 and the Swiss Automobile Club (ACS) (031) 328 3111, offer a breakdown service. If your car is hired, follow the instructions.

PERSONAL SAFETY

Switzerland is generally a safe place for tourists, with the greatest risk coming from tourists, but to help prevent crime:

- Do not carry around more cash than you need.
- Do not leave valuables at the poolside.
- Beware of pickpockets in tourist spots or crowded places.
- Avoid walking alone at night in dark alleys in large cities.

Switzerland has several police forces, with a federal force as well as cantonal ones. If you need a police station ask for *die Polizei* (in German-speaking parts), *la Police* (French) or *la Polizia* (Italian).

Police assistance:
☎ **117**
from any call box

TELEPHONES

Public telephones take both coins and cards (PTT phonecards). Coins from 5 centimes to 2 francs can be used, but the minimum amount for a local call is 60 centimes, Sfr 1 for a national call, and Sfr 5 for an international call. Phonecards of various values can be obtained from post offices and many shops. Calls are usually more expensive from hotels.

The cheap rate for calls 18.00–08.00 hrs Monday to Friday, and all day Saturday and Sunday.

The country code for Switzerland is 41.

International Dialling Codes	
from Switzerland to:	
UK:	**00 44**
Germany:	**00 49**
USA:	**00 1**
Netherlands:	**00 31**

POST

Main town post offices (*Postamt* in German, *la Poste* in French, *la Posta* in Italian) are open Monday to Friday 8:30–6:30, Saturday 8:30–11; smaller ones close for lunch.

Correspondence can be forwarded to Swiss post offices for collection – clearly mark the envelope 'Poste restante', and make sure you put the postcode before the name of the town. To collect a letter the addressee should produce his/her passport as proof of identity.

ELECTRICITY

The power supply in Switzerland is 220 volts. Sockets accept two-round-pin plugs, so an adaptor is needed for most non-Continental appliances and a transformer for appliances operating on 100–120 volts.

TIPS/GRATUITIES

Yes ✓ No ✗		
Restaurants (usually included)	✓	10%
Cafés/bars	✓	Change
Tour guides	✓	3 francs
Taxis (usually included)	✓	10%
Porters	✓	2 francs
Chambermaids	✓	2 francs
Usherettes	✓	Change
Hairdressers	✓	Change
Cloakroom attendants	✓	Change
Toilets	✗	

PHOTOGRAPHY
What to photograph: buildings in the old town centres, alpine villages, mountains, the magnificent views
Best time to photograph: all day. The mountains look especially good in early morning light and at sunset.
Where to buy film: films and camera batteries are readily available in tourist and photographic shops.

HEALTH

Insurance
Switzerland does not have a state health system so visitors are strongly advised to take out medical insurance.

Dental Services
There is no state dental service so visitors are strongly advised to take out medical insurance that covers dental care.

Sun Advice
In southern Switzerland especially the summers are hot so visitors should take precautions against the sun. In winter the sun is stronger than it seems because of the altitude of most winter sports resorts, so again take precautions against burning.

Drugs
Medicines for personal use only are allowed through customs. Many prescription and non-prescription drugs are available from pharmacies.

Safe Water
Swiss tap water is completely safe to drink. However, because of the sterilisation processes many people buy mineral water, which is readily available everywhere.

CONCESSIONS

There are no special student or senior citizen concessions on offer in Switzerland. Discounted travel cards are available to all.

CLOTHING SIZES

USA	UK	Europe		
36	36	46		
38	38	48		
40	40	50		Suits
42	42	52		
44	44	54		
46	46	56		
8	7	41		
8.5	7.5	42		
9.5	8.5	43		Shoes
10.5	9.5	44		
11.5	10.5	45		
12	11	46		
14.5	14.5	37		
15	15	38		
15.5	15.5	39/40		Shirts
16	16	41		
16.5	16.5	42		
17	17	43		
6	8	34		
8	10	36		
10	12	38		Dresses
12	14	40		
14	16	42		
16	18	44		
6	4.5	38		
6.5	5	38		
7	5.5	39		Shoes
7.5	6	39		
8	6.5	40		
8.5	7	41		

Land of Contrasts

CANTONS

Switzerland is a federation of 23 states, or cantons (to be precise there are 20 cantons and six half-cantons), each of which has its own constitution and legislature. Twenty two cantons were established in 1815 with the 23rd canton, Jura, formed in 1978. The Swiss citizen is primarily a member of a 'communite' (commune), of which there are over 3,000, active within the structure of the cantons forming the Swiss Confederation. Both commune and canton are self-governing.

Within this landlocked country there are such distinctions that it seems barely credible they are contained in so small a place. A journey of just 160km takes you from the rolling, tree-clad hills of the Jura through Mittelland, a low-lying, pastoral landscape whose towns have ancient hearts but modern outlooks, to the Alps, where Europe's highest mountains are found. Add a handful of lakes and some great rivers and you have a combination that offers the finest panoramas. And, if you add a few more kilometres to your journey, it can include villages where four distinct languages are spoken.

There are many good reasons to visit Switzerland. Its location in the heart of Europe means that Switzerland's heritage is a fascinating blend of European cultures, histories and traditions. But there is more to Switzerland than glorious scenery; you'll find excellent museums, fine food, sophisticated resorts, health spas, dynamic sports and an excellent rail system. It's compact, so the cities, towns, villages and incomparable natural wonders are all easily accessible. Where trains and cars can't go, cable cars and boats will get you there and with 60,000km of hiking trails and nine national bicycle routes extending over 3,300km you can soon get off road.

Lac Léman (Lake Geneva) is the largest lake in Alpine Europe and Switzerland is the birthplace of the Rhine,

Zürich's Bahnhofstrasse

Europe's longest river. Sixty per cent of Switzerland is covered by the Alps and the Swiss Alps have more 4,000m peaks than any other country and boast two of Europe's most famous mountains, the Eiger and the Matterhorn.

Natural beauty confronts you at every turn. From the imposing, snow-covered peaks of the Jungfrau to immense glaciers eroding Alpine valleys and the dazzling array of colour to be found in the flower-rich meadows, there is always something special. Scenic beauty is not confined to the uplands of the Alps and the Jura, however; the low-lying land between the mountain ranges, studded with tranquil lakes and lush pastures, offers a peaceful contrast. The Swiss care intensely for the environment: not only the countryside but the streets of villages and towns are clean and well-kept.

Take time to explore. Switzerland is not best seen in a hurry – take a walk in the mountains, seek out the medieval heart of an old town or relax by the shores of a lake. From world-famous mountain resorts and stunning glaciers to traditional villages and winding valleys and gorges, the variety of landscape makes Switzerland a very special destination.

hang-gliding is the best way to see Switzerland's diverse landscape

POWER TO THE PEOPLE

The power given to the individual citizen of Switzerland is best seen when the Federal Assembly, which sits in the capital Bern (► 36) passes a law. If 50,000 people sign a petition against the law a national referendum must be held. As the Swiss are proud of saying, this system gives them the right to say 'No' when Bern says 'Yes'.

Rock climbing

History

200 BC
What is now Switzerland is settled by the Helvetii, a Celtic tribe from east of the Rhine. They in turn are driven out by the Alamans.

1st century AD
Switzerland becomes the Roman province of Helvetia.

5th century
Following the fall of the Roman Empire western Switzerland is settled by the Burgundians, while the Alamans recover the east.

530
The Franks conquer Switzerland. Later the country forms part of Frankish Charlemagne's Holy Roman Empire.

11th–13th centuries
After the fall of the Frankish Empire Switzerland is divided between Germanic noble families, one of which is the Habsburgs.

1191
Bern founded.

1264
Count Rudolf III of Habsburg gradually wins control of most of Switzerland.

Sixteenth-century Protestant reformer, Jean Calvin

16

1291
Rudolf dies and though he leaves his Swiss holdings to his sons, the three original 'forest' cantons of Schwyz, Unterwalden and Uri agree an alliance to resist Habsburg domination. The document, on which the alliance is recorded, names the Confederation of Helvetica. The famous story of William Tell and his apple shoot is set during the struggle for independence.

1315
The Confederation defeats Duke Leopold's Habsburg army at the Battle of Morgarten.

1386
The enlarged Confederation defeats the Habsburgs at the Battle of Sempach.

15th century
The Confederation is enlarged and, by signing treaties with Austria and France and fighting against the Italians, consolidates its borders.

16th century
The Reformation sweeps through Switzerland. In 1536 Jean Calvin flees from Paris to Genève, the city then becoming the centre for Calvinism.

I. CALVIN

1618–48
Switzerland remains neutral during the Thirty Years War. Neutrality is confirmed at the Münster Conference of 1648. Though the country is necessarily involved in the Napoleonic conflicts, this sets the seal on Swiss neutrality.

1798
France occupies Switzerland and dissolves the Confederation.

1803
Napoleon reforms the Confederation, but Genève and the Valais (Wallis) remain French. Napoleon builds a road over the Simplon Pass.

1815
The Congress of Vienna re-establishes Switzerland with 22 cantons, and also cedes the Swiss part of the French Jura to the Swiss. Swiss neutrality is reaffirmed, and later guaranteed in Paris.

1846–48
Religious divisions result in the Sonderbund War, a civil war of limited fighting. The war ends with the adoption of a new constitution that creates a federal state of 22 sovereign cantons and introduces central secular rule.

1864
The Geneva Convention codifies the 'rules' of war, and the Red Cross is formed, both on initiatives of Jean Henri Dunant.

1914–19
The Swiss remain neutral throughout World War I. After the war the League of Nations is set up in Genève.

1939–45
Switzerland remains neutral during World War II. In subsequent years Swiss neutrality makes it a favoured place for international organisations.

1978
Jura becomes the 23rd canton.

1992
Switzerland decides not to join the EC, but does become a member of the IMF and the World Bank.

1995
The International Trade Organisation is formed, based in Genève.

2000
Switzerland is declared a full member of the United Nations.

The headquarters of the International Trade Organisation in Genève

Flora & Fauna

VIEWING THE FAUNA

The best places to see indigenous wildlife at close quarters are the parks and nature reserves. Of these, the huge Swiss National Park in the Grisons stands out as an exceptional monument to the extraordinary beauty and power of nature.

Irrespective of the season, the Alps offer an extraordinarily rich and varied collection of flora but it is in the spring and summer that the mountainscape comes alive with colour. In the valleys early Alpine flowers are hidden from view beneath taller plants but, progressively, they reappear at higher levels as the snows recede up the mountainside. By late summer only the most resilient species of high-Alpine flora are still found, and these tend to congregate almost exclusively by the snowline. Above the tree line, the scree slopes and loose moraines are the highest habitats supporting plant life before the bleak mountainscape of permanent snow and ice is reached. Here, in inhospitable surroundings, flowering plants contrive to exist and flourish in freezing conditions – covered for over half of the year by a blanket of snow.

With the thaw in late April and early May, the slopes burst into riotous colour with sturdy Alpine snowbells pushing their way impatiently through the melting snow. Following their example, coltsfoot, crocuses and spring gentians make their first appearance – the latter studding the mountainsides with their distinctive blue flowers. Large blooms and deep shades of colour are distinctive features of Alpine flora, a factor which is entirely due to the increased ultraviolet content of light at high altitude.

Vibrant Alpine flowers

If the Alpine zone offers the most dramatic of settings for flora, it is unquestionably the lower-lying meadows that offer the greatest variety in the most tranquil surroundings. Against the impressive background of white peaks and glaciers, these pastures – grazed by cattle during the summer – provide an exquisite mosaic of contrasting colours. Bellflowers, daisies, knapweeds, bladder campions,

Ibexes on Mount Pilatus in Central Switzerland

Fire lillies thrive in the rugged glacial environment of the Sustenpass with snow-topped mountains beyond

yellow monkswood and hay-rattles proliferate, and in damp hollows, clumps of butterworts amd marsh marigold lend an extra splash of colour. Burnt orchids and the creamy spikes of elder-flowered orchids are also widespread, and in mid-summer the round-headed and black vanilla members of the species add to the variety. Not surprisingly with such a banquet of flower heads on offer, the air hums with insect life in search of nectar. Butterflies are numerous; blues, skippers, fritillaries, apollos and whites flutter dreamily among the changing colours.

The animal and bird life of the Swiss Alps is largely similar to that of other central European countries. Alpine marmots, large rodents with coarse fur, are ubiquitous, their burrows lining mountain paths or set in tussocks of grass in meadows. Alpine swifts are often seen swooping around rocky cliffs, while high above the peaks, golden eagles, peregrine falcons and griffon vultures can occasionally be seen circling. The Alpine chough is the most commonly seen bird at high altitude. Distinguished by their yellow beaks and red claws, their inquisitive nature has given them a virtual monopoly of mountain restaurants.

Among the larger animal species found in the Alps, the chamois are the most abundant of those living at high altitude. The rarer ibex is also occasionally seen. At lower altitude roe and red deer proliferate. In winter, skiers are often surprised by the sight of ermine stoats scampering across the piste and very occasionally, polecats and foxes will be seen prowling through trees.

DISAPPEARING EDELWEISS

The most famous Alpine plant is the edelweiss, sadly far too frequently victim to collectors – not withstanding its protected status. Its distinctive white 'fur' is seen less and less throughout the Alpine region, and is increasingly supplanted by the no less appealing dwarf willows, saxifrages and sandworts, Alpine toadflax and moon daisies often sprouting from clefts in rocks.

The People

The Swiss have a reputation for being an aloof, even cold people, but that is a misunderstanding. They are an efficient people – the buses and trains run on time – and such an ordered way of life can be misinterpreted by visitors. But behind the well-organised and structured society is a kind, welcoming people. The Swiss are also keen on their health, often putting welfare first when considering changes, for instance banning cars from parts of inner cities. The visitor benefits from all these aspects, whether on the ski slope, which will be well groomed and reached by good lifts; on a walk, which will be well signed; in the pedestrian-only town centres; or in the clean, well-run hotels. Forget your preconceptions – Switzerland is a beautiful place and the Swiss will do their best to help you enjoy it to the full.

Although Switzerland has more annual visitors per capita than any other country in Europe, very few of them ever leave with more than the faintest understanding of the country or the people they have visited. Even long-term foreign residents in Switzerland rarely develop more than the most rudimentary knowledge of their host country's system of government, its political creed, or even the 'national character' – if such a thing exists. The majority of the 6.9 million population is concentrated in the predominantly German-speaking Mittelland, the vast central plateau north of the Alps stretching from the French to the Austrian

SWISS TALK

It would be wrong to suppose that most Swiss have a reasonable grasp of each of their official languages. Within a few miles you can move from an exlusively German-speaking communtiy to one where only French is spoken. It is also a myth that all Swiss speak English, although most people employed in service industries have at the very least a moderate grasp of the language.

Zürich's China Garden

Left: *night torch procession in Engelberg valley*
Below: *traditional Zermatt costumes*
Bottom: *parade in Zurich*

border. Well over half the population is involved in the service industries such as banking and tourism, with much of the remainder working in the chemical and pharmaceutical industry, machine tool production and watchmaking; only a tiny percentage are now involved in agriculture.

A striking indication of the heterogenous population structure is the multilingual character of the country. For 74 per cent of Swiss the first language is German, 20 per cent speak French, 4 per cent Italian and the remaining 2 per cent Romansch. All four Swiss languages are officially recognised throughout the country, and although standard German is deemed to be the formal language of government, in fact the preferred alternative is 'Schwyzerdutsch' or 'Swiss-German'.

As much in the banking houses of Zürich (➤ 32–3) as in the remotest of mountain hamlets, the outlook of the Swiss people has been shaped largely by economic and political necessity. This has made them pragmatic, instinctively cautious, and prudent. It has also made them ingenious in the use of the few natural resources they have. Their lives demonstrate intelligence, industriousness, discipline, thrift, a Teutonic love of order (mixed with an equal amount of Latin flair), independence of mind, and a commitment to quality and craftsmanship that make their products highly valued throughout the world.

FIRST TOURISTS

Modern tourism began in Switzerland and hospitality is a long-standing tradition. As early as the mid-19th century well-to-do Victorians were starting to visit the country and with the expansion of the railways once isolated villages grew into popular resorts. Skiing, climbing, hiking and visits to health spas became very popular and the Swiss people soon developed resorts to accommodate the growing numbers.

Food & Drink

Switzerland has no lack of good restaurants offering a wide choice of specialities. There is not really any such thing as Swiss cuisine but the regional foods and dishes are nourishing, wholesome and often country-style. Visitors can experience a fascinating variety of tastes and influences concentrated within a relatively small area. Each of the 23 cantons have their own regional foods. Specialities include Neuchâtel tripe; *Berner Platte*, a Bernese dish of boiled meat and sausages served with haricot beans; *rösti*, grated fried potatoes; St Gallen sausages (*Bratwurst*); *papet* (leeks with potatoes) from the canton of Vaud; Ticinese risotto; Basel's brown-flour soup (*Mehlsuppe*) and onion flans; Zürich's shredded veal (*schnitzeltes Kalbfleisch*); barley soup and air-dried meats (*Bundnerfleisch*) from the Grisons; and of course all the cheeses – Gruyère (*Greyerze* in German and *Groviera* in Italian), Emmentaler, Appenzeller, Jura, the French-Swiss *tommes*, and the herb cheeses from Eastern Switzerland, plus the famous cheese dishes: fondue, *raclette* and cheese flans. Although these foods have originated from various regions of Switzerland, some dishes are instantly recognised all over the world as 'Swiss'. Switzerland is synonomous with fondue, *rösti*, meringues, zabaglione, muesli, Emmental and Gruyère cheeses and the celebrated chocolates of Nestlé, Lindt and Tobler. The Swiss also know a thing or two about cooking, their master chefs have earned a reputation throughout the world's great kitchens.

WINES AND SPIRITS

Switzerland has eight wine areas and as many vintners as there are sunny slopes for growing grapes. The major areas are Genève (red and white wines), Neuchâtel and Vaud (white), the southern Valais (white Fendant and red Dôle), the Ticino (red Merlot), and the Grisons (red Veltliner). Fruit brandies are a popular Swiss speciality.

Swiss cheeses are best in fondues

You shouldn't overlook the many fish dishes, the endless varieties of bread, the red and white wine specially chosen to go with each of these dishes, the range of spirits, Kirsch, Williamine, marc and grappa, and the ciders and mineral waters. Vineyards have been cultivated in Switzerland since Roman times and despite its highs and lows over the centuries, Swiss wine is today offering some top quality red and white. Then there are the cakes and confectionery: *cuchaules* and *taillaules* (breads eaten on Sundays), butter cakes and *bricelets* from the French-speaking part of Switzerland, Kirsch gâteau from Zug (➤ 59), Unterwalden's scrambled pancakes, pear bread from central Switzerland, carrot gâteau from Aargau, *Leckerli* honey biscuits from Basel (➤ 30–1), Bernese meringues, and nut cake from the Grisons.

It is important to note that a 'menu' is *Karte* in German-speaking Switzerland and *carte* in the French-speaking part. If you ask for a 'menu' the waiter is more likely to return with the dish of the day, since that is what the word means to the Swiss. All *Karten* have a *menu*, which is usually the chef's special at a moderate price; this may also be listed as *Tagesplatte*, *Tagesteller* or *plat du jour*, depending on whether the language is German or French.

chocoholics are in for a treat when they visit Switzerland

SWISS CHOCOLATE

The Swiss are famed worldwide for their chocolate. In addition to the well-known names of Tobler, Nestlé and Lindt & Sprüngli, look out for the products of gourmet chocolatiers such as Moreau, found in the Neuchâtel region, and Zürich-based Teuscher.

Customs & Folklore

RE-ENACTMENTS

Despite Switzerland's known neutrality in recent wars, historical festivals commemorating many of the Confederation's great battles are held throughout the year.

In common with mountain dwellers throughout the world, the descendants of the original Alpine inhabitants are tough, stoical, resourceful and inherently superstitious. Many of the surviving rituals, therefore, have their roots in a form of obeisance to the unpredictable nature of the brooding mountains that surround them. Other rituals are designed to deter evil spirits from their valleys, ensure the fruitfulness of their lands, appease the harsher elements of the weather, and invest in fulsome gratitude for a bountiful harvest. These ancient Alpine rituals are frequently characterised by a rich assortment of grotesque masks and outlandish costumes, particularly in harvest festivals. However, it is the most significant dates on the Christian calendar that really set the streets of Alpine towns and villages alight. Christmas and New Year are quiet, but the periods of Lent, Holy Week and Corpus Christi are marked by colourful processions and carnivals throughout the Alps. Later in the year, arguably the most impressive religious spectacle of all takes place in the monastic town of Einsiedeln (► 51) where a torchlight procession winds through the streets in celebration of the Miraculous Dedication.

White Turf St. Moritz: horse-races are held on the first three Sundays in February

The summer calendar in the Alps is characterised by pastoral festivals, cows are bedecked with colourful ribbons and flowers entwined around their horns, their cow-bells jangling and accompanied by traditionally dressed herdsmen. Through the summer, music and arts festivals are held in many of the more fashionable resorts such as Montreux (► 65). With the onset of autumn, grape festivals are held throughout the wine-making regions, and the season is also the time when some of Switzerland's best-known markets are held – most notably the famous Onion Market in Berne (► 36–7).

SWISS ANTICS

During a long tourist season there is no shortage of opportunities to witness at least one Alpine festival and, in so doing, to ponder on one of the enduring paradoxes of Swiss life. It is a source of continuing bemusement to foreign visitors that an ordinarily undemonstrative people should indulge in their public spectacles with such uncharacteristic abandon.

Calendar of Events

January

Folk celebrations in most towns and villages to usher in the New Year; horse-racing on snow in St Moritz and Arosa; the Vogel Gryff festival in Basel; International Lauberhorn ski races in Wengen.

February/March

Famous Basel carnival, beginning on the Monday after Ash Wednesday; Fritschi-Fasnacht festival in Luzern, starting on the Thursday before Ash Wednesday; procession of harlequins in Schwyz; Mardi Gras in the Ticino; speed skating championships in Davos.

March/April

Engadine cross-country ski marathon; Parsenn Derby downhill ski race at Davos; footwashing ceremonies on Maundy Thursday in numerous Catholic communities; religious processions in many southern towns on Good Friday.

April

Festa delle Camelie at Locarno; Sechseläuten festival of Zürich, featuring a parade and bonfire; blessing of horses, donkeys and mules at Tourtemagne on 23 April; start of the Primavera Concertistica classical music festival in Lugano.

May

Festival of the Feuillu on the first Sunday in May at Catigny, Genève; procession headed by the Grenadiers of God at Kippel, in the Valais; Spring Musical Festival in Neuchâtel; beginning of festival of music and ballet in Lausanne; Golden Rose Television Festival at Montreux.

June

Rose Week in Genève; International June Festival in Zürich; Art Festival in Bern; High Alpine ballooning at Mürren.

July

Rose Festival of Weggis; crossbow shooting in the Emmental; giant slalom on the Diablerets' glacier and summer ski race on the Jungfraujoch; International Jazz Festival of Montreux; Nyon Folk Music Festival.

August

Swiss National Day celebrations throughout the country on 1 August; Genève Festival, featuring fireworks and parades; music festival in Luzern and film festival in Locarno; folk festivals at Interlaken; Yehudi Menuhin festival at Gstaad.

September

Shooting contest in Zürich; torchlight religious processions at Einsiedeln; music festival in Montreux (also at the end of August and beginning of October).

October

Garden show in Genève; agricultural and dairy show at St Gallen; Italian Opera Festival in Lausanne; vintage festivals in wine-growing regions.

November

Numerous open-air markets throughout Switzerland, that at Bern, the Zibelemârit (onion market), being one of the most fascinating.

December

Internationally famous ice-hockey tournament in Davos; Escalade, an ancient custom, in Genève on 11 and 12 December, with torchlight processions; numerous festivals on St Nicholas Day, 6 December.

SWITZERLAND

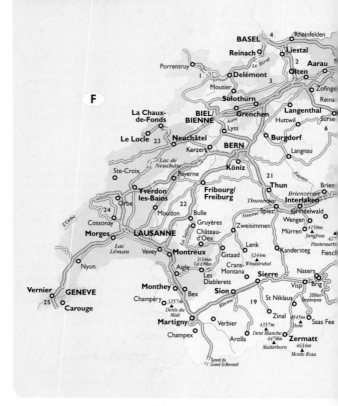

BASEL 4 Rheinfelden
Reinach Liestal
Porrentruy 2 Aarau 5
1 Delémont Olten
Moutier 3 Zofinge
Solothurn Reina
La Chaux- BIEL/ Grenchen Langenthal
de-Fonds BIENNE Huttwil Surse
Aare Lyss 6
Le Locle 23 Neuchâtel Burgdorf
Kerzers BERN
Langnau
Lac de Köniz
Ste-Croix Neuchât Payerne 21
Thun Brien
Yverdon- Fribourg/ Brienzersee
les-Bains Freiburg Thunersee Interlaken
Orbe 22 Simme Spiez Grindelwald
Cossonay Moudon Bulle Zweisimmen Wengen 4158m
Gruyères Mürren Jungfrau 42
Morges Château- Finsteraarh
Lac d'Oex Lenk Kandersteg Fiesc
Léman Vevey Montreux Gstaad 3244m
Nyon Aigle 3154m Windstrubel
Col d Pillon Crans- Naters
Vernier Monthey Les Montana Sierre Visp Brig
GENEVE Diablerets St Niklaus 2006m
25 Bex Sion Simplonpass
Carouge Champéry 3257m 19
Dents du Zinal 4545m
Midi Rhône Dent Blanche Dom Saas Fee
Martigny Verbier 4357m
Champex Arolla 4478m Zermatt
Matterhorn 4634m
Tunnel du Monte Rosa
11 Grand St-Bernard

F

L'Orbe

La Sarine

Lac
Léman

14 Schaffhausen
15 Appenzell Auserrhoden/
   Appenzell Innerrhoden
16 Grisons/Graubünden
17 Ticino
18 Uri
19 Valais
20 Obwalden
21 Bern
22 Fribourg
23 Neuchâtel
24 Vaud
25 Genève

Northern Switzerland

Zürich, the country's biggest city, is the focal point of German-speaking Switzerland, which occupies much of the northern part of the  country. The northeast borders the Bodensee, fringed by attractive towns and villages, while the gateway to the strategically important northwest is the fascinating city of Basel (Basle), noted for its carnival and wealth of monuments and museums. Other key atractions include the medieval spa town of Baden and the Schaffhausen set on the River Rhine, close to the German border.

St Peter's church in Zürich

ℹ Bahnhofstrasse
☎ 50 056 222 5318

Historisches Museum
✉ Landvogteischloss
☎ 056 222 7574
🕐 Tue–Fri 1–5, Sat–Sun
10–5
👋 Cheap

BADEN

This health resort is worth visiting for its delightful location in the foothills of the Jura even if you are not interested in 'taking the waters'. Known in Roman times as Aquae Helveticae, its hot curative sulphur springs, gushing forth at 48°C (118°F), have, over the centuries, attracted people seeking relief from rheumatism and respiratory disorders. The resort is well equipped with excellent hotels and pleasant parks, as well as a casino. Baden's picturesque old town, the core of the medieval settlement, has much of interest, including a covered wooden bridge (Holzbrücke) built in 1810 that leads across the River Limmat to the old governor's residence, now housing the **Historisches Museum** (Historical Museum). Here you'll see displays of pottery from the area, antiques, armour and excavated coins.

The spa itself is attractively laid out, with pretty gardens, and facilities include indoor and outdoor tennis courts, fishing, and an open-air swimming pool. The Limmatpromenade along the river is a pleasant walk.

ℹ Aeschenvorstadt
☎ 36 061 268 6868

Kunstmuseum
✉ St Alban-Graben 16
☎ 061 206 6262
🕐 Tue–Sun 10–5
👋 Moderate (free Sun 4–5)
🍴 Café

Museum für Gegenwartskunst
✉ St Alban Rheinweg 60
☎ 061 206 6262
🕐 Tue–Sun 11–5
👋 Moderate (free Sun 4–5)

Basel Zoo
✉ Binningherstrasse 40
☎ 061 295 3535
🕐 Mar–Oct: daily 8–6 (6:30
May–Aug). Jan–Feb,
Nov–Dec: 8–5:30
👋 Expensive
🍴 Café

BASEL (BASLE)

Switzerland's second-largest city is as full of variety as you would expect. The university, founded in 1460, is Switzerland's oldest and perhaps most prestigious; the numerous museums and art galleries are known far and wide; and fascinating old buildings and a wealth of monuments lend the city dignity and charm. Yet Basel is also a lively, progressive place, a financial and industrial centre, renowned not only for its stores and boutiques but also for its outstanding research and conference facilities. The Swiss Industries Fair alone accounts for over one million visitors a year.

Basel has managed to preserve most of its fine old town. The view of the cathedral, with its two spires, from the right bank (Kleinbasel) is particularly impressive, as is that from the Pfalz (cathedral promontory) back over Kleinbasel. Then there are the picturesque Gothic sections of town with magnificent fountains, the market square in front of the imposing Rathaus (town hall) and the

The collection at Basel's Kunstmuseum dates from 1662

Spalentor, the city's western gateway and reputedly the most beautiful in Switzerland.

Basel's extensive range of museums houses some of the world's most prestigious collections of old and new masterpieces. The - **Kunstmuseum** (Museum of Fine Arts) is the pride and joy and is said to be the oldest

Vincent van Gogh's Le Jardin de Daubigny *is among the paintings in the Kunstmuseum*

public art collection in the world, dating from 1662. It is rich in old masters such as Witz, the Holbeins, Grünewald and Manuel, as well as great collections of 19th- and 20th-century art. The **Museum für Gegenwartskunst** (Museum of Contemporary Art) is widely recognised as Europe's leading museum of art of the 1960s, 1970s and 1980s. It features such artists as Frank Stella, Donald Judd, Bruce Nauman, Richard Long and Jonathan Borofsky.

Basel's other fine monuments include the Münster (Cathedral), founded in 1019 by the Emperor Henry II; the Historisches Museum housed in a 14th-century Franciscan church; the Predigerkirche or Dominican Church (1269); the Rathaus (town hall) of 1504–14; and town mansions and corporate houses from the 15th and 16th centuries. Also worth a visit is **Basel Zoo,** just a short walk from the railway station. Here, some 5,500 animals and 600 different species live in a magnificent park in the middle of the city.

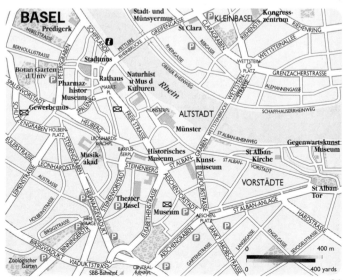

i Fronwagplatz 4
☎ 052 625 5141

Museum zu Allerheiligen
✉ Klosterstrasse
☎ 052 633 0707
🕐 Tue–Sat 12–5 (Thu until 8), Sun 11–5
💵 Free

SCHAFFHAUSEN

Capital of Switzerland's northernmost canton, Schaffhausen, set on terrraces on the right bank of the Rhine, contains some of the country's most impressive ancient buildings. The majority of these 16th- to 18th-century buildings – embellished with statues, reliefs, frescos and oriel windows – are found in the old town centre, which is a pedestrian-only zone. In the public squares are historic fountains, and no fewer than 12 guildhalls, some now restaurants, that attest to the prosperity of their masters. The ancient heart of the town was the street market, in what is now the Vordergasse. Presiding over all is St John's Church, noted for its excellent acoustics. Music lovers delight in its Good Friday concerts and the Bach Festival held every three years.

The **Museum zu Allerheiligen** (All Saints' Museum) contains a notable cultural and historical collection, including prehistoric collections from local excavations. For great views of the town and the surrounding area visit the circular Munot Fortress. The top of the fortress is reached by climbing a spiral ramp inside the keep.

i Hauptbahnhof
☎ 01 215 4000

Musée Swisse
✉ Museumstrasse 2
☎ 01 218 6511
🕐 Tue–Fri 10:30–5
💵 Cheap
🍴 Café

A fine view of Zürich looking across to the Alps in the background

ZÜRICH

Although Switzerland's largest city is small by world standards, with a population of around 400,000, it nevertheless boasts all the advantages of an international metropolis, together with an attractive location at the northern end of Lake Zürich (Zürichsee). Switzerland's most important centre of commerce, banking and industry – silk, cotton, machinery, paper and food – Zürich is also a main cultural centre of German-speaking Switzerland. The best way to get to know the attractive old town is on foot. The Lindenhof is a good starting point and offers an attractive view over the old town and a chance to see ruins of a Roman fort. The modern city silhouette is dominated by the striking towers and spires of three old churches – the Grossmünster, endowed by Charlemagne; St Peterskirche, with Europe's largest clock face (8.6 metres), and the Fraumünster, admired for its stained-glass windows by

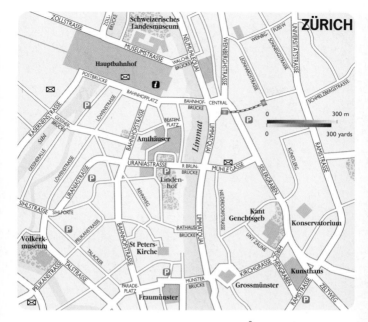

Marc Chagall (completed 1970). By far the prettiest area in the town is around St Peterskirche and the Fraumunster, with alleys and attractive squares from where you cross the delightful Munsterbrucke (bridge) to reach Grossmunster. A milestone in Zürich's development into an important international financial, economic and trade centre was the foundation of the Zürich Stock Exchange (Börse) in 1877.

More than 30 museums in Zürich offer a great variety of exhibitions; the many interesting exhibits in the **Musée Suisse** (Swiss National Museum) opposite the main railway station, for example, offer a lively demonstration of Swiss history. The municipal theatre (Schauspielhaus), the Opera House (Opernhaus), the Concert Hall (Tonhalle) and various smaller theatres as well as other institutions offer a varied selection of cultural events. Culture is highlighted in the annual June Festival, whose concerts, opera, ballet, drama, exhibitions and lectures, all centre on a particular theme. Full details of events appear in the *Zürich Little Big City What's On*. For those in search of nightlife, nightclubs are numerous and range from the fashionable to the folkish.

Zürich's international reputation also rests on its excellent shopping facilities and its fame as an art-dealing centre. Bahnhofstrasse, with its elegant boutiques and couturières, is one of the most attractive shopping streets in the world and has the unusual distinction of a catacomb of bank vaults beneath it.

Fireworks on New Year's Eve

33

Bernese Oberland

The second largest of Switzerland's cantons, the 6,050sq km area is more than two-thirds mountainous with the great rocky spine of the Bernese massif traversing the area from the Wildhorn range in the west to the Sustenhorn on the border with central Switzerland. The southern flanks of these great mountains form part of the neighbouring canton of Valais, but the magnificent peaks of the Jungfrau, Eiger, Mönch and Finsteraarhorn are all part of the Bernese Oberland. Here also is Bern (Berne), an enchanting city with its distinctive blend of medieval beauty and quiet charm.

Giessbachfall, Brienz

ℹ️ Dorfstrasse 23
☎ 033 673 8080

ADELBODEN

A quaint old village at the head of the broad, sunny valley of Engstligental, Adelboden lies below the towering 3,243m Wildstrubel on the western extremity of the Bernese Alps. To the east it is well-sheltered by the 3,049m Lohner. At 1,356m it is one of the Bernese Oberland's highest altitude resorts and, since its link with the nearby ski resort and spa town of Lenk (▶ 43), it has moved progressively up the league of Switzerland's winter sports resorts. It retains a traditional Alpine feel with an attractive cluster of ancient timber houses leaning precariously into the street. A popular summer resort since the mid-19th century, there are many delightful walks around Adelboden, through Alpine pastures richly carpeted with rhododendrons – particularly above the small hamlet of Boden.

ℹ️ Im Bahnhof, Bahnhofplatz
☎ 031 328 1212

Kunstmuseum
✉ Hodlerstrasse 8–12
☎ 031 328 0944
🕐 Tue–Sun 10–5 (until 9 Tue)
💵 Moderate
🍴 Café-bar

Schweizerisches Alpines Museum
✉ Helvetiaplatz 4
☎ 031 351 0434
🕐 Tue–Sun 10–5, Mon 2–5
💵 Moderate
🍴 Snackbar

Naturhistorische Museum
✉ Bernastrasse 15
☎ 031 350 7111
🕐 Tue–Fri 9–5, Sat–Sun 10–5, Mon 2–5
💵 Cheap
🍴 Café

BERN (BERNE)

In 1848 Bern had the honour of being chosen by the first Swiss parliament as the capital of the Swiss Federation. By European standards it is not a large city but it is archetypically Swiss and picturesque. The secret of the city's enduring appeal is that is has little of the functional architecture that blights other historic capitals. Since the 1950s Bern has expanded enormously, and bridges now span the Aare to link the old city with its new suburbs. While retaining its medieval appearance, the old city (Nydegg) has developed into an major business centre.

Characteristic of Bern's streets are the medieval arcades set into the façades of the buildings. Even in the worst of weathers you can walk from one end of the old city to the other without getting your feet wet. Bern guards its arcades with a jealous eye; no house may be rebuilt or renovated without an arcade on the ground floor, and every façade has to fit in with neighbouring ones. High above the rooftops towers the Münster (Cathedral of St Vincent), one of the finest ecclesiastical buildings in Switzerland. Like most of Bern it dates from the 15th century. The cathedral dominates the curve of the Aare, where the steep ramparts of the old walls plunge down to the river. The Zeitglockenturm is one of Bern's most popular attractions. Originally dating from the 12th century, it was gutted in 1405, and then rebuilt in stone. In 1530 the astronomical or calendar clock, showing the position of the sun, moon, stars and planets as well as the month and day of the week, was constructed. Below the Cathedral is Junkerngasse containing the houses of the old city aristocracy. Rathausgasse – with its beautiful late Gothic town hall dating from 1406 – and Postgasse, which broaden out virtually into extended squares, and Kramgasse and Gerechtigkeitsgasse, with their magnificent 16th-century fountains, each with a theme, run parallel to it. On Holderstrasse the **Kunstmuseum** (Fine Art Museum) is one of the best art galleries in Switzerland and has a particularly fine collection of works by Paul Klee.

The new town, across the Aare, is accessible by four bridges. Of special interest here is the Bundeshaus (Federal Palace), a domed 19th-century Florentine Renaisssance-style building. The new town is home to several museums including the **Schweizerisches Alpines Museum** (Swiss Alpine Museum), which highlights the natural history and culture of the Swiss Alps, including the history of mountaineering. Close by are the communications museum, the museum of Bern and the **Naturhistorische Museum**, one of the major natural history museums in Switzerland.

Left: *arcades cover the high street and adjoining side-streets of Bern*

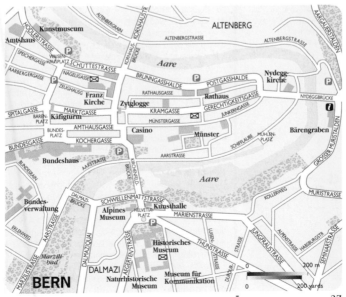

Traditional wooden houses

🛈 Hauptstrasse 143
📞 033 952 8080

Ballenberg Open Air Museum
📞 033 951 2030
🕐 Daily 10–5 mid-Apr to Oct
💲 Expensive
🍴 Restaurants

BRIENZ

Nestling between the upper end of Lake Brienz and the southern slopes of the Brienzer Rothorn, Brienz is 15km east of Interlaken (► 40–1). At 568m above sea-level Brienz enjoys a mild mountain climate thanks to the compensating effects of the lake. The village is known for its local craft of wood-carving.

From the Brunngasse up to the old church, the village centre has been well preserved, its wooden houses in the narrow alleys ablaze with pelargoniums in the summer, while the lakeshore promenade is a delight. The lake itself is excllent for swimming, waterskiing, sailing, surfing or fishing, or you can enjoy a trip on one of its famous paddle-steamers. Alternatively, follow walks up into the mountains and explore villages along the lake. **Ballenberg Open Air Museum**, northeast of the village, has old farm buildings and houses that you can explore, plus farm animals and demonstrations of traditional crafts.

🛈 Sportzentrum
📞 033 854 1212

GRINDELWALD

Popularly known as the 'village of the glaciers', Grindelwald sits on a broad, sunny plateau some 1,050m above sea-level. The most famous and largest ski resort in the Bernese Oberland, the town is a gateway to the whole Jungfrau region with an enormous choice for intermediate and advanced skiers. In winter the car park close to the railway station is used as an ice rink and for ice sculptures.

As you walk away from the station up the long main street you see the Alpine-style buidings framing the Wetterhorn.

Grindelwald Mountain Walk

Take the three-stage gondola lift from Grindelwald up to the summit of First, past the splendid Oberer Glacier descending between the Wetterhorn and Schreckhorn to the right, and take the path signed Bachsee. After a slightly steep beginning this is a lovely walk of about an hour along a fairly level path, forking right along the northern bank of a tiny lake, to the edge of Bachsee itself.

Turn left along the northern shore of the lake following the signs for Waldspitz. This is a gradual descent of about 40 minutes, through a few scattered farm buildings where there is a choice of paths – each leading to the restaurant at Waldspitz. From here follow the main path down through a forest to a sharp left turn after about 15 minutes. Continue down through the trees, bearing left until the landscape opens up and the path leads through a meadow beneath the First gondola, just south of the Bort lift-station.

Weary walkers can return by lift at this point. Otherwise the hour-long descent continues through pleasant Alpine pastures with magnificent views of the glacier. The path curves round to the right towards Milibach, and after about 10 minutes it reaches a crossroads where there is a surfaced track leading left. Continue straight ahead until the path rejoins the track at Milibach. Shortly it joins a narrow road, from where it is approximately a 15-minute walk back down to the bottom lift-station.

Distance
17.5km
Dashed section 4.5km
Time
Allow 3 hours

Grindelwald is a wonderful place to visit in summer, with guided Alpine walks a popular option. Mountain bikes are also available. For tennis fans there are open-air courts; and the sports centre's ice rink, open for skating from July to April, is also used for tennis in May and June. The sports centre, centrally located, also offers a sauna and solarium, fitness facilities, table tennis, a children's play area, a casino and an indoor pool.

39

Interlaken Town Walk

Distance
5.5km
Time
Allow up to 2 hours

Tourisk Museum
✉ Obere Grasse 28
☎ 033 822 9839
⏰ May to mid-Oct: Tue–Sun 2–5
💷 Cheap

Start at the town's casino, the Kursaal, on the north side of the splendid Höheweg. The Kursaal (1) is a curious hybrid of architectural influences; this rambling building dates from the mid-19th century. Walk north up the Strandbadstrasse and over the bridge to the Goldey Promenade. Turn left along the river bank, passing the huge lido on the right, and continue along the leafy Untere Goldey. Turn right at the end up the Beatenburgstrasse and then left into Auf dem Graben. Here is the Gothic Church, Unterseen (2), an imposing building particularly notable for its magnificent mountain backdrop.

Continue down the Auf dem Graben and then turn left into the Obere Gasse, which features the **Tourisk Museum** (3). Housed in a fine 17th-century house, this small regional museum records the history of the town and the development of the Jungfrau region.

Walk east down the Untere Gasse, turning right over the bridge into the Spielmatte on a narrow island in the middle of the Aare. Cross over another bridge and walk down the busy Marktgasse to the Postplatz. Turn left here and walk east into the famous Höheweg. Cross the road and walk along the shady Hohe-Promenade, passing the palatial hotels on the left. Turn right into the Peter Ober Alle, which bisects the Höhematte (4), the delightful 14-hectare central park. At the end of the park turn left into the Spielplatz on the southern perimeter of the Höhematte and continue walking east through a shady avenue. Bear round

🛈 Höheweg 37
☎ 033 822 2121

INTERLAKEN
Set between the sparkling waters of Lake Thun and Lake Brienz, Interlaken enjoys a magnificent setting on the

The flower clock and the casino in the gardens of the Kursaal which also has a theatre and a cafe

to the left, leave the park, and cross the north-bound Klosterstrasse, and view the former Augustinian Monastery (5). On the right side of the Klosterstrasse, traces of the 12th-century priory remain in the Protestant church of St Mary. The adjacent castle, now the cantonal administration centre, is a mid-18th-century baroque structure.

Return to the Klosterstrasse and turn right. Turn left at the top, back on to the Höhe-Promenade, and then cross the Höheweg, turning right up the Strandbadstrasse back to the Kursaal.

Street market in Interlaken

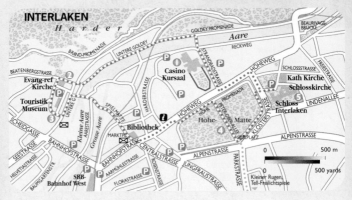

banks of the River Aare. One of Switzerland's longest established holiday resorts, Interlaken lies at an altitude of 568m and offers a wide range of sport, entertainment and excursions in the surrounding area. The Jungfraujoch and its famous railway station – the highest in Europe – or the Schilthorn, with its mountaintop revolving restaurant are just two possible trips.

The main promenade, the 'Höheweg' (known as the 'Höhe'), is lined with flowers and fronted by a huge open meadow from where you can enjoy one of the most famous views in the world – that of the Eiger, Monch and Jungfrau. The mountains' names derive from an old legend about how a wily monk saves a young woman from the clutches of an ogre. Although a long walk from the town centre Höheweg is where you'll find the better, more fashionable shops as well as many hotels, a selection of restaurants and tea rooms, plus the Kursaal Casino.

The village of Kandersteg lying at the foot of rugged escarpments, which frame the snow-peaks of the Blumlisalp to the east

JUNGFRAUJOCH

This shoulder of the Jungfrau peak is both a monument to Swiss ingenuity and a confirmation of the awesome beauty of their mountain home. It merits the former accolade because it is made accessible by a miracle of engineering, and the latter because of the panorama that rolls out beneath its unique belvedere. Europe's highest railway station is here, cut into the rock at an altitude of 3,475m in eternal snows. It has three restaurants, an ice palace, an observatory that is part of an Alpine research station; from the Sphinx Observation Terrace the views of the Aletsch Glacier (Europe's longest) and the Mönch and Jungfrau defy description.

A leisurely walk through the Ice Palace, deep inside a glacier, is a memorable experience, but, understandably, warm clothing is advisable if the fascinating sculptures are to be appreciated in comfort. In summer the Jungfraujoch has a celebrated ski school, and dog-sleigh rides are available throughout the year, weather permitting. A word of caution: when visiting Jungfraujoch you'll need to walk slowly to avoid headaches brought on by the altitude.

KANDERSTEG

Popular for its dramatic setting in glorious mountain scenery, Kandersteg is a major mountaineering and winter sports centre at the head of the Kandertal Valley. Above it to the southeast are the great peaks of the Doldenhorn, Fründenhorn, Oeschinenhorn and Blümlisalp, a huge mountain group streaked by impressive glaciers. To the southwest lie the smaller, but no less striking, peaks of Lohner and Bundespitz behind which lies Adelboden, about 8km as the crow flies.

 Dorftstrasse
☎ 033 675 8080

In summer it has all the usual amenities associated with a major Alpine resort. Nearby, the Oescheninsee, accessible part way by chair lift from the centre of the village, is a beautiful mountain lake set in an amphitheatre of imposing mountains and glaciers. The walks around the lakeside are strongly recommended.

LENK

A splendidly sited resort in a wide sunny basin at the head of the Simmental Valley, Lenk is a health and winter-sports resort famed for its sulphurous springs and rugged, glacial scenery. The village is a successful symbiosis of the old and new, with flower-decked chalets softening the sharp lines of some extensive new development. Excellent for walkers, there are more than 200km of hiking trails in the area. One of the chief attractions is the town's proximity to two fine waterfalls, the Iffigenfälle (Iffigen Falls) and the Simmenfälle (Simmen Falls), 4km south and southeast respectively from the centre. Both involve short walks at the end of good mountain roads where there is ample car parking. For the Iffigen Falls there's a walk of about 20 minutes up a steep track; the Simmen Falls, thundering down the northern face of the impressive 3,243m Wildstrubel, is only about 5 minutes from the car park.

🛈 Rawilstrasse 5
☎ 033 733 3131

MEIRINGEN

The town is the main tourist centre of the precipitous Haslital Valley, east of Lake Brienz. Many of its buildings were destroyed in two serious fires in the late 19th century, but the church of St Michael, rebuilt in 1684, survived along with a few wooden houses. Meiringen is said to be where the name for meringue originated after a pastry cook made one for Napoleon.

Meiringen is a time-honoured excursion centre for a number of reasons. The famous Reichenbach Falls, immortalised as the place where Sherlock Holmes and Moriarty were believed to have plunged to their deaths, are just to the south of the town. If you are lucky, you'll see salamanders at the falls. A funicular leaves from a station to the right of the road to the Grimselpass. The eery Aareschlucht (Aare Gorges), an impressive cleft through limestone cliffs, are also on the southern outskirts of the town just before Innertkirchen. Viewing galleries are located at various stages along its course.

🛈 Bahnhofstrasse 22
☎ 033 972 5050

Below: *the fast-flowing River Aare rushing through the Aare Gorge*

The funicular descends towards the village over the rooftops of Mürren. The area offers spectacular views across the summits of the Jungfrau range, here obscured by clouds

🛈 Sportzentrum
☎ 033 856 8686

MÜRREN

Set in a superb position on a mountain terrace facing the Jungfrau and the Eiger, Mürren has long been a popular choice with winter-sports enthusiasts, even though the choice for skiing is not as great as in some of Switzerland's bigger resorts. At an altitude of 1,638m it is the highest and most impressively sited village in the Bernese Oberland. It is traffic free as no roads lead to the resort, the village being reached, instead, either by funicular from Lauterbrunnen or by Schilthorn cable car from Stechelberg. There are easy nursery slopes in the centre of the village, and beginners are taken up to Allmendhubel with its gentle slopes and a drag lift to make things easier. There are special classes for children from three years of age.

It is a very picturesque, unspoilt village which, with its wooden chalets and narrow winding alleys, has great charm and character. The Schilthorn towers above the resort and at its 3,048m summit there is a superb revolving restaurant which was featured in the James Bond film *On Her Majesty's Secret Service*.

Other facilities include a leisure centre with indoor pool, whirlpool, squash courts, gymnasium, ice rink and a library, and there are also indoor tennis courts, a sauna and solarium, as well as a network of paths for walking.

Mürren Mountain Walk

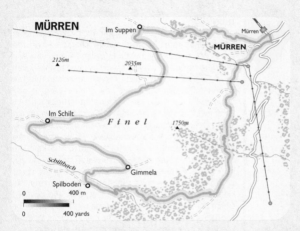

From Mürren's upper road, facing the old funicular station up to the Allmendhubel, turn left and then right after about 100m up the mountain path signposted Im Suppen and Blumental. At a junction after 10 minutes or so take the lefthand path signposted Im Suppen. This is a gentle and pretty climb of just under 1km through trees to a delightful mountain restaurant. From here follow the path south to Im Schilt, climbing beneath the Birg cable car, then across broad pastures with stunning views over the Lauterbrunnen Valley to the Jungfrau massif.

Bear left at the huddle of farm buildings at Im Schilt, and follow the path down to some more farm buildings at Gimmela. Take the right-hand path down to Spilboden, crossing a small bridge over the Schiltbach, and then walking along its southern bank for about 300m to a sharp left turn. Recross the Schiltbach almost immediately and continue down past barns and storehouses on the left, keeping ahead at the next junction, and then enter a dense thicket from where the path emerges to rejoin a larger track that descends to the bottom station of the Birg cable car. From there it is a 10-minute walk back to the centre of the village.

Distance
7km
Time
Allow 2 hours

Stunning Staubbach falls, a silvery leap of 305m from a ledge beneath the village of Mürren

Bahnhof
☎ 033 222 2340

Sunlight strikes the castle at Oberhofen that juts out into the reflective waters of Lake Thun

THUN

Located on Lake Thun this ancient and picturesque town has retained much of its medieval character over the years, which, combined with its delightful mountain and lakeside setting, makes it a worthy rival to Interlaken (► 40–1) as a suitable base for excursions within the Bernese Oberland. The hill, the Schlossberg, is still crowned by a spectacular four-turreted fortress, built by Berchtold V of Zähringen after 1182. In the town on the street Obere Hauptgasse, look out for the extraordinary arrangement of paved walks actually on the roofs of the shops. The town has two delightful parks. The Jakobshübeli, south of the town centre on the eastern bank of the Aare, is a hilly, densely wooded public space with marvellous views reached by steps from the Hofstettenstrasse. Across the river, over the covered Obere Schleuse bridge, is the Schadau Park laid out in the mid-19th century in the style of the great parks of Victorian London. It is especially notable for its splendid castle.

Steamers operate to towns and villages around Lake Thun. Other attractive towns and villages to visit include Interlaken to the east; Oberhofen, noted for its medieval

castle; Spiez on the south shore with its impressive castle and museum; and Gunten on the north shore with its lakeside lido.

WENGEN

Wengen is a perfect place for relaxing and unwinding – there is very little to disturb the peace, not even a road up from the Lauterbrunnen Valley. Instead, everyone and everything comes here by the mountain railway that continues on up to Kleine Scheidegg and the Jungfraujoch and which also links Wengen with Grindelwald (▶ 38–9). The resort's real advantage is the direct access to the whole Jungfrau region, by means of either the mountain railway to Wengernalp or the cable car to the top of the Männlichen from where there is an enormous choice of runs. Wengen has had a long association with the British, and there is even an English church.

🚹 Dorfstrasse
☎ 033 855 1414

Wengen's quiet streets and parks are perfect for a relaxing visit

In summer Wengen offers many walks around the village, along a network of paths that take you through mountain woods and flower-filled meadows with views of the Jungfrau Glacier and over the valley to the Schilthorn. This is some of the best walking country in Switzerland. You can take the railway up to Kleine Scheidegg at the foot of the Eiger and walk back down to Wengen.

WILDERSWIL

This is a picture-postcard village with lush green fields and meadows and traditional old chalets decked in summer with pink and red pelargoniums. The village is an ideal starting point for easy walks through the meadows and on the lower mountain slopes. Wilderswill has been inhabited for more than 1,000 years and for centuries the mill was a popular meeting place. Today, the **Alte Mühle** (old mill museum) hosts temporary exhibitions devoted to local culture, arts and crafts and village life. It is possible to walk in a couple of hours to the peaceful little resort of Bönigen on Lake Brienz with its narrow streets and attractive chalets. Not to be missed is a trip on the rack-and-pinion railway that leads up from Wilderswil to the famous Alpine Garden at Schynige Platte.

🚹 Lehngasse
☎ 033 822 8455

Alte Mühle
✉ Wilderswil
☎ 033 251 1169
🕐 May–Oct: Thu
7:30pm–9:30pm; Sat 5–7;
Sun 10–12; (also Wed
7:30pm–9:30pm, Jul–Aug)
🎟 Free

47

Central Switzerland

The region of central Switzerland has proved to be a powerful lure for visitors to the country since the very beginning of the Swiss tourist industry. Long before the winter-sports boom, the majority of the early tourists headed directly for the ancient city of Luzern (Lucerne) and its immediate environs. It was, and remains, incontestably the finest excursion centre in the Swiss Alps. The city and its canton, and the neighbouring cantons of Uri, Schwyz, Unterwalden (divided into the half-cantons of Obwalden and Nidwalden) and Zug, not only form the physical heart of Switzerland, but also represent the historical embryo of the modern Confederation.

Breathtaking valley view in the Klausen pass from Linthal to Altdorf

Tellspielhaus,
Schützengasse 11
☎ 041 872 0450

Tell-Museum
✉ Bürglen
☎ 041 870 4155
🕐 May–Oct: daily 10–11:30,
1:30–5 (9:30–5:30
Jul–Aug)
💰 Cheap

Above: *Cruise ships with
music and dancing call at
Brunnen on Lake Luzern*

Bahnhofstrasse 32
☎ 041 825 0040

ALTDORF

The capital of Uri canton, Altdorf lies in a fertile valley on the main St Gotthard Pass route. It is a charming, old-fashioned town closely associated with the legend of William Tell who is said to have accomplished his feat of apple-splicing here. In Altdorf's narrow streets, the architecture of many of the 17th- and 18th-century houses show decidedly Italian influences – a reminder of the important commercial significance of the town's location. Close to Altdorf are three villages of considerable charm. In Seedorf is a Benedictine monastery with a decorative baroque chapel. Nearby is a little 16th-century gabled castle, A Pro. The ancient and picturesque settlement of Bürglen, 3km southeast, is reputed to have been the birthplace of William Tell, and the **Tell-Museum** is housed here in an old medieval tower. Bauen, 10km north, is a delightful little hamlet on the west bank of Lake Uri directly opposite Tell's chapel.

BRUNNEN

Brunnen, on the shore of Lake Luzern and framed by mountains, is a resort with characteristic Swiss houses and shops and a lakeside promenade complete with attractive cafés. Look out for the gaily painted water pumps dotted around the village, and be sure to visit the pretty little chapel in the centre of town. The resort has a lido where you can bathe in the lake or swim in the indoor pool.

Steamers from Brunnen call at historic sites on the lake such as William Tell's chapel and the Rütli meadow, birthplace of the Swiss Confederation. For evening entertainment, cruises with music and dancing are popular, or you can try your luck in the casino. Live bands perform throughout the summer, and every week a Swiss folklore evening is held with Alpine music.

BÜRGENSTOCK

Less of a community and more of a massive and luxurious hotel complex, Bürgenstock is also the name given to a cliff rising abruptly from the southern bank of Lake Luzern. On a plateau at about 500m is a purpose-built holiday resort created by Franz Joseph Bucher-Durrer at the end of the last century. Today it is still privately owned, and the palatial hotels have become a popular and exclusive retreat for the fashionable and famous.

Not least of the resort's attractions is a magnificent panorama of the lake, the distant Jura, and Luzern's twin sentinels of Rigi and Pilatus. There are many footpaths through woods and Alpine pastures, and an excellent circular cliff path – the Fersenweg – which is about a half-hour walk around the mountain. At the midway point is the highest and fastest mountain lift in Europe, which ascends, intermittently through the cliff-face, to the Hammetschwand at a height of 1,128m, taking less than a minute. The view from the summit is magnificent, and there is a small restaurant and a couple of bars from which to enjoy it. Bürgenstock can be reached by car or by funicular in eight minutes from Kehrsiten at the lakeside.

EINSIEDELN

Known as the 'jewel' of the Schwyz canton, this is a summer and winter resort of special appeal. Its site is particularly beautiful, deep in a basin in the green ring of the lower Alps with their rugged foothills, rolling meadows and dark, scented pine forests. However, its fame springs chiefly from its reputation as one of western Europe's most important places of pilgrimage and the huge Benedictine monastery, rebuilt between 1704 and 1735, dominates the town. Here in August one of the greatest Swiss religious festivals, the celebration of the Miraculous Dedication, takes place.

The town of Einsiedeln lies below the monastery and is surrounded by glorious countryside of pleasing contrasts. The peaks of Nüsellstock, 1,479m, and Gschwandstock, 1,616m, lie immediately to the south with the lake and pleasant pasturelands of Sihlsee to the east. Many of the fields are occupied by horses bred by the monks – a tradition that dates back to the 15th century.

🛈 Burgenstock Hotels & Resort
☎ 041 612 9915

Below: golden statue of the Virgin Mary in the square fronting the Benedictine monastery, Einsiedeln

🛈 Hauptstrasse 85
☎ 055 418 4488

Klosterstrasse 3
☎ 041 639 7777

Right: Lucerne's 14th-century Kapellbrücke (Chapel Bridge) spanning the River Reuss, the older Water Tower stands to the left

The Titlis mountains, the highest viewpoint in Central Switzerland

ENGELBERG

Dominated by a 12th-century Benedictine monastery, this pretty village is at the foot of the Titlis mountains at the heart of a beautiful valley that leads up from Lake Luzern. It is a charming spot with a relaxed atmosphere. The Titlis Glacier means that it can boast snow year-round – you can usually even enjoy limited skiing here in July! There are over 56km of downhill runs in three areas, with something for all grades of skier. The run from Titlis to the village is about 13km long. A free ski-bus service takes about three minutes to transport you from the village to the gondola cable car that takes you up to Gerschnialp at 1,250m, from where two further cable cars run parallel up to Trubsee at 1,800m. From Trubsee a two-stage cable car rises to nearly 3,000 metres. The second stage has the novelty of the world's first rotating cabin, allowing thrilling views of the dramatic glacial scenery.

The village has a good range of additional facilities, such as indoor skating and curling rinks, two tennis courts, swimming pools, tea rooms and plenty of excursions, as well as guided tours of the monastery, making it a popular resort during the summer too. There are many miles of excellent marked paths around Engelberg.

LUZERN (LUCERNE)

Luzern may lack the cosmopolitanism of Zürich (➤ 32–3), Genève (➤ 62–3) or Bern (➤ 36–7), but it is the most delightful of Switzerland's cities, small enough to be walked round easily and with good restaurants, shops and sightseeing possibilities, coupled with a magnificent setting. Standing in the foothills of the St Gotthard Pass, Luzern borders the lake of the same name, which winds deep into the Alpine ranges of central Switzerland. Here, the gentle waterscape contrasts with wild, majestic scenery and, not surprisingly, a lake excursion is a must.

Seeing Luzern on foot is a joy. You can stroll alongside the River Reuss and marvel at the Kapellbrücke (Chapel Bridge), built in 1333. When the bridge is lit at night it is the most romantic place in Switzerland. With its numerous gable paintings and sturdy water tower (once part of the town's defences), it is the city's unmistakable landmark. The southern end of the Kapellbrücke is close to the railway station and near the northern end are quaint alleys and enchanting medieval buildings. In the city's arcades, on Tuesdays and Saturdays in particular, you can enjoy the hustle and bustle of the market crowd as you shop. The attractive railway station is next to a stunning **Culture and Convention Centre**, which includes a huge concert hall, designed by French architect Jean Nouvel and completed in time for the new millennium.

The popular **Verkehrshaus der Schweiz** (Swiss Transport Museum) on the lakeside is reached from the town centre by car, bus or ferryboat. The museum traces the history, development and importance of transport on land, water and in the air and is one of the largest and most comprehensive collections of its kind in Europe. Other popular museums include the **Historisches Museum** (Historical Museum) and the **Picasso Museum**.

Luzern boasts a wide range of sporting opportunities, from freshwater beaches to scenic golfing, with annual horse-races and rowing regattas on the Rotsee. The Fritschi-Fasnacht celebrations (➤ 25) are increasingly popular: several days of parades, concerts and dancing culminate with a huge concert lasting into the early hours.

🛈 Bahnhofstrasse 3
☎ 041 227 1717

❓ Lake Luzern Navigation company has large comfortable steamers (hourly departures; some services have a restaurant) whose range of half- or full-day excursions can be combined with a trip to the top of a mountain

Culture and Convention Centre
✉ Europaplatz 1
☎ 041 226 70 70

Verkehrshaus der Schweiz
✉ Lidostrasse 5
☎ 041 370 4444
🕐 Apr–Oct: daily 9–6.
Nov–Mar: 10–5
💷 Expensive

Historisches Museum
✉ Pfistergasse 24
☎ 041 228 5424
🕐 Tue–Fri 10–4, 2–5;
Sat–Sun 10–5
💷 Cheap

Picasso Museum
✉ Furrengasse 21
☎ 041 410 3533
🕐 Apr–Oct: daily 10–6.
Nov–Mar: 11–1, 2–4
💷 Cheap

PILATUS

The mount of Pilatus is one of the attractions of the Swiss Alps. The huge pyramid of rock, 2,132m tall, presides like a massive watchtower over Luzern some 15km to the northeast. Detached from the main range of the Alps, it stands as a solitary giant in the centre of the country, and its forbidding precipices and jagged peaks have been the source of countless legends over the centuries. No visit to this part of Switzerland is truly complete without making the rewarding ascent to its summit. The ascent can be made in a number of ways: by foot from Hergiswil – a gruelling 5-hour climb of about 1,700m; 40 minutes by gondola lift from the suburb of Kriens, changing to a cable car at Fräkmüntegg; or the most popular route by the steepest cogwheel railway in the world, from Alpnachstad, a small village on the lakeside. In 1868 Queen Victoria ventured to the summit on the back of a mule but, sadly, this form of transport is no longer available. The rack railway, built between 1886 and 1889, is a remarkable engineering achievement. The total length of track is 4.5km with a minimum gradient of 19 per cent and a maximum of 48 per cent (or nearly 1 in 2) – said to be the steepest in the world. The journey up to Pilatus-Kulm takes about half hour each way.

From the top station it is a short walk to either of the two peaks of Esel or Oberhaupt up steep, well-prepared paths and steps. The openings in the Oberhaupt tunnel offer glorious views of Lake Luzern, spread-eagled far below with the surrounding countryside laced with silver, thread-like rivers. The highest projection of the mountain, the Tomlishorn, can be reached in under half hour by a scenic cliff path. In all directions the panorama is overwhelming. To the north the view extends over the Swiss lowlands, dotted with sparkling lakes, to the Black Forest; to the east, over the lake and beyond Rigi (► 55), the Säntis range; to the south and west, the ice-capped giants of the Bernese Oberland.

RIGI

Some 21km east of Luzern, the mighty 1,797m-high cliffwall of the Rigi is as enchanting and friendly as Pilatus (► 54) is stern and forbidding. Separated by Lake Luzern, the two mountains have vastly different personalities, with Rigi traditionally earning greater affection from local people. In the 19th century it became the goal of every tourist in Switzerland, doubtless lured by tales of spectacular sunrises and magnificent views. Then, many of them had to be turned away from the limited number of mountain inns and hotels; today, there are countless hamlets and small resorts scattered about the mountainside – detracting little from its considerable appeal. The main resort is Rigi-Kaltbad, some 300m beneath the summit and reached by cable car from the charming lakeside resort of Weggis (► 58–9), or by railway from Vitznau (► 58). The latter is the oldest railway of its type in Europe, built in 1871. It continues up to the resort of Rigi Kulm, the mountain's highest point, which is also accessible by mountain railway from Arth-Goldau, inaugurated four years later. Both journeys take about 35 minutes. From this point the radius of the remarkable view stretches about 150km in clear weather. There are many delightful, easy walks through Alpine pastures and, in winter, some fine intermediate skiing.

Below: *the cable car to Rigi-Kaltbad rises high above the resort of Weggis*
Bottom: *railways connect some of the highest villages on Rigi*

ℹ Hofstrasse 2
☎ 041 666 5040

SARNEN

The historic capital of the forest canton of Obwalden, Sarnen is situated at the northern end of the pretty lake of Sarnersee, in the middle of the lush Alpine pasture between Interlaken (▶ 40–1) and Luzern (▶ 53). Conspicuous on a hill above the town to the southwest the twin-towered parish church of St Peter, founded in the 11th century, dates in its present form from 1742. The Town Hall houses the 'White Book', the earliest record of the Swiss Confederation.

The Melchtal is a fertile pastoral valley leading south from Sarnen to the tiny resort of Melchsee-Frutt on the bank of the Melchsee. Cable cars at various points along the valley assist hikers taking the mountain route to Engelberg (▶ 52).

ℹ Bahnhofstrasse 4
☎ 041 810 1991

SCHWYZ

The ancient town of Schwyz, capital of its canton, gave its name to Switzerland. The town has one of the most ornate rural baroque churches in the country as well as other noteworthy buildings dating to the 16th century, some of which belong to families that trace their roots back to the founding of the Confederation. The Rathausplatz is one of the best in the country, cobbled and ringed by 17th and 18th century Alpine houses with dormer windows. Don't miss the splendid pre-World War II Bundesbriefarchiv on the Bahnhofstrasse where the collection of federal documents dates from the 13th century. The excellently preserved 14th-century banners are impressive. The building itself is decorated, inside and out, with some unusual frescos painted in the 1930s.

The town is in a beautiful position at the foot of the twin peaks of the Mythen, rising to a height of 1,811m and 1,899m respectively. To the west is the Urmiberg, the eastern spur of the Rigi, and to the east the truncated cone of the Fronalpstock.

The ancient town of Schwyz

Schwyz Cycle Tour

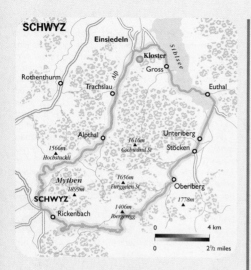

Distance
46km (28.5 miles)

From the Hauptplatz in the centre of Schwyz, turn left by the side of St Martin's Church and ride through the village of Rickenbach, about 1.5km southeast. This winding mountain road gets steeper as it makes its tortuous way through thick forest for about 10km to the viewpoint of Ibergeregg at 1,406m. The most difficult part is now over. From here the road descends steeply at first, then more gently by the right bank of the Minster to the tiny hamlet of Tschalun. At the village of Oberiberg just ahead, follow the main road northwest through Stöcken and Unteriberg.

Continue around the southern tip of the Sihlsee, follow the east bank through Euthal and cross over the bridge on the left just past it. Turn right at the end and continue along the lake's west bank through Gross. Turn left into the centre of Einsiedeln (► 51). Pass the monastery on the left, bear right into the main street and take the first road on the left to Alpthal. This crosses over the Alp River just before the village of Trachslau, and then climbs along the river's west bank to Alpthal where, at the end on the right, a bridle-path climbs steeply to the Haggenegg Pass. You might need to dismount for this part. The climb lasts a little over 3km, but from Haggenegg the path rejoins a mountain track for the 6km descent to Schwyz. (If the Pass does not appeal, return to Schwyz on the main road from Einsiedeln via Biberbrugg, Rothenturm and Sattel.)

Seestrasse
☎ 041 398 0035

Festung Vitznau
☎ 0041 398 0035
🕓 May–Oct: Fri 5 (guided tours). Groups of 10 or more can book all year
💷 Expensive

VITZNAU

This charming lakeside village is situated below Mount Rigi. Here, the oldest cog railway in Europe ascends to Rigi Kulm. The station at Vitznau is idyllic: close to the lake shore and only a couple of minutes' walk from the jetty, from where you can board a steamer and visit the beauty spots along Lake Luzern's shores. The village has a relaxed atmosphere with a lakeside promenade, colourful cafés and *stüblis*. Join one of the guided village walks arranged by the local tourist office.

An interesting feature of Vitznau is the **Festung Vitznau** (artillery fortress), constructed inside the cliffs of the Rigi as part of the Gotthard defence during World War II. For many years it was a well-kept secret and it was always operational. In 1998 the fortress was decommissioned and is now open to the public. You can join a guided tour and see munitions depots, tunnels and the soldiers' living quarters. You can even spend the night in the fortress, sleeping as soldiers do in Swiss Army sleeping bags and eating a genuine Swiss army breakfast. Details are available from the Vitznau tourist office.

Seestrasse 5
☎ 041 390 1155

WEGGIS

This little resort with its flower-decked promenades, lakeside lido and mild, sunny climate is about 40 minutes by lake steamer from Luzern (▶ 53).

Looking through a gap in the bankside trees towards Lake Luzern. A pretty fountain sprays water into a small pool in the foreground

A good spot for a relaxing break, Weggis offers a variety of leisure facilities including a heated indoor swimming pool, outdoor tennis courts, fishing, sailing and windsurfing. Each morning in the summer season you can enjoy a concert on the lakeside bandstand or in one of the hotels. In July 1998 a marina was opened in the picturesque bay at Lüzelau.

There are numerous walks in the hills behind Weggis and concerts and folklore evenings are held throughout the summer. The 'Rose Festival', hosted each year by Weggis and including music, dancing and a fireworks display, takes place the last weekend in June.

ZUG

Alpenstrasse 14
☎ 041 711 0078

On the banks of the second largest lake in central Switzerland, the Zugersee, Zug is an ancient walled city with a well-preserved medieval centre distinguished by ruined fortifications and delicate spires. This is clustered around the old Kolinplatz. On the side of the square is the 16th-century Rathaus (town hall) and a fine old clock tower (the Zytturm) with a blue and-white tiled roof crowned by a slender belfry. The picturesque rows of houses in the Ober-Altstadt and Unter-Altstadt between the Kolinplatz and the lake date from the 16th century, and to the east up the Aegeristrasse is the 1526 Capuchins' Tower, close to the 16th-century chapel of a Capuchin convent. The other medieval tower of interest is the Pulverturm (Powder Tower) on the southern extremity of the old town on the Zugerbergstrasse.

The town's most outstanding structure is the late-Gothic church of St Oswald, just to the south of Kolinplatz. Built between 1478 and 1515, it is dedicated rather curiously to the English saint Oswald – it is said his remains were brought to Zug at the time of its foundation. The choir stalls date from 1484. The handsome church of St Michael, on a hill to the east, was erected in 1902.

The quaysides from the Seestrasse to the Alpenquai offer delightful views of the mountains, including Rigi (► 55) and Pilatus (► 54), and the peaks of the Bernese Oberland. The town's own mountain, the 1,039m Zugerberg, is a tall, wooded plateau reached by car through the Schonfels, southeast of Zug. From there it is a short climb to a terrace with impressive views.

Lac Léman

The crescent-shaped Lac Léman (Lake Geneva) shares its banks between France and Switzerland – the latter having roughly two-thirds of the shoreline. Most of the Swiss lakeside is on the sunny north bank in the canton of Vaud and the exclusive strip of land between Lausanne and Montreux has come to be known as the Swiss Riviera. But the wider Lac Léman region is no less appealing, with its blend of sloping vineyards, atmospheric towns and villages, and stunning waterscapes across the lake to the Savoy Alps of France. Thanks to the Alps, which tower above it to the east and the Jura that bounds it to the west in the direction of France, the Lac Léman region has always offered outstanding opportunities for visitors.

Ouchy, one mile from Lausanne, on the north shore of Lac Léman

ℹ Rue du Mont-Blanc 18
☎ 022 909 7000

Musée d'Art et d'Histoire
✉ 2 rue Charles-Galland
☎ 022 418 4600
🕐 Tue–Sun 10–5
🎫 Free
🍴 Café

Musée de l'Horlogerie
✉ 15 route de Malagnou
☎ 022 418 6470
🕐 Wed–Mon 10–5
🎫 Free

**Musée International de la
Croix-Rouge et du
Croissant-Rouge**
✉ Avenue de la Paix 17
☎ 022 748 9511
🕐 Wed–Mon 10–5
🎫 Moderate
🍴 Café

*Cathédrale de Saint-Pierre
towers over the old town*

GENÈVE (GENEVA)

Framed by the Alps and Jura mountains, Genève sits on the shores of Lac Léman, the largest Alpine lake. Lakeside promenades and flower-filled parks are typical of this city, while the lake supports leisure activities as well as water taxis. Large steamers offer longer trips – the most popular passing the palatial homes of film stars and business magnates. The Jet d'Eau, a towering spray of water over the lake, is Genève's landmark.

This major hub of European cultural life is an important international meeting venue, convention and exhibition centre, and a major financial, commercial and industrial city which attracts more visitors than any other Swiss city.

The lower town, lying between the south bank of the Rhône and the old town, is the main business and shopping quarter, notable for shopping in rue du Rhône rue de la Corraterie. In place Neuve are two of Genève's landmarks, the Grand-Théâtre, one of Europe's most opulent opera houses, and the Conservatoire de Musique.

Don't miss the old town's art galleries, antique shops, bookshops and bistros. Dominated by the Cathédrale de Saint-Pierre, the real centre is the place du Bourg-de-Four, dating back to Roman times and probably the oldest square in the city. Internationally important excavations under the cathedral show that the site dates from AD1000 and has yielded evidence of early Christian life and art. The cathedral was constructed in the 12th century in a mixture of Romanesque and Gothic styles. To the right of the main entrance the 15th century 'La Chapelle des Macchabées' was built in flamboyant Gothic style. Over the centuries the cathedral was ravaged by fire and rebuilt on several occasions.

The Hôtel de Ville in Grand-rue, is also part of Genève's old quarter. The façade of this rather austere building was

begun in 1617 and finished only at the end of the 17th century, a third floor was added in the early 19th century. The vast and elegant courtyard has a ramp leading up to each floor. The International Red Cross was founded here in 1864. Next to the town hall, on the esplanade known as La Treille, is a large square tower built in the latter half of the 15th century and known as the Tour Baudet. On the other side of the street is the former arsenal built in the first half of the 17th century for use as a granary.

Among the best parks are the Jardin Anglais on the left bank, notable for its flower clock; and the Parc de la Grange, with a beautiful rose garden, the site of the annual international competition of new roses.

Among Genève's 30 museums are the **Musée d'Art et d'Histoire** (Museum of Art and History), housing Egyptian, Greek and Roman works of art, a coin collection and Swiss furniture exhibition; the **Musée de l'Horlogerie** (Watch and Clock Museum) has a rare collection of 16th- to 20th- century enamelled, decorative clocks, watches and music boxes; the **Musée International de la Croix-Rouge et du Croissant-Rouge** (Museum of the Red Cross and Red Crescent), which explores the history of the movement.

Museum of the International Red Cross with the sculpture Les Petrifies *by Carl Butcher*

63

Avenue de Rhodanie 2
☎ 021 613 7373

Musée des Beaux Arts
✉ Palais de Rumine, Place
de la Riponne 6
☎ 021 316 3445
🕐 Tue–Wed 11–6, Thu
11–8, Fri–Sat 11–5
💰 Cheap

Musée Olympique
✉ Quai d'Ouchy 1
☎ 021 621 6511
🕐 May–Sep: daily 9–6 (Thu
until 8). Oct–Apr: Tue–Sun
9–6 (Thu until 8).
💰 Expensive
🍴 Restaurant

*Lausanne's port is at
Ouchy, about a mile
from the town*

LAUSANNE

Sitting halfway along the north bank of Lac Léman, Lausanne has a strongly individual charm but enjoyment of that charm takes a little effort – from Ouchy on the lakeside to the highest point of the city is a stiff climb of about 235m. A convenient little railway runs from the city centre (place St François) down to Ouchy, the city's port, where young and old throng the pavement cafés and restaurants and stroll round the boat quays. This is where the Lac Léman steamers come alongside.

The successors of the inhabitants of Roman Lousonna gradually moved from the lakeside up the slopes, settling in places that could be better defended. On these ridges, where the Cité now stands, arose the Bishop's Palace and the stately Notre Dame Cathedral, consecrated in 1275. One of the finest Gothic buildings in the country, it is one of the last places in the world to still have the tradition of the night watch.

Built at the end of the 14th century and the beginning of the 15th, Château St Maire is now used as the seat of the canton government. Around this nucleus grew the modern city. Today, bridges link the various parts of Lausanne. Above and below the bridges are houses clinging so closely to the hillsides that they have entrances on several levels.

The Palais de Rumine (Rumine Palace) built at the beginning of the 19th century, houses Lausanne University and several museums covering fine arts, history, natural history and botany. Of particular interest is the **Musée des Beaux Arts** (Museum of Fine Art) with its collection of Swiss art and excellent contemporary art exhibitions. The **Musée Olympique** (Olympic Museum) traces the history of the Olympic Games.

The headquarters of the Federal Court, the International Committee for the Olympic Games and the many international fairs and congresses have given Lausanne an international reputation. Many of the exhibitions and other events take place in the Palais de Beaulieu where there is also one of the biggest and most modern of Switzerland's theatres. And it is here that every year from May to July for the past 24 years, well-known artists of the world of music and dance have gathered together.

MONTREUX

Since the 18th-century writer Jean-Jacques Rousseau chose Montreux as the setting for his novel *La Nouvelle Héloise*, the town has developed into one of the most popular and populated places on Lac Léman. Its position is superb, on a wide bay open to the south, with wooded hills and sloping vineyards to the rear protecting the whole area from north and east winds. The lake stores the heat, reflects the light, and makes Montreux's climate delightful. The wealth of trees and plants, some of them subtropical, on the quais, make a paradise for strollers between Clarens and Chillon Castle. Fig and almond trees flourish, as do laurels and eucalyptus; there are cypresses, magnolias and palm trees, and every spring the whole town resembles a masive bouquet, with its higher-lying pastures covered with thousands of narcissi.

Apart from its wide modern streets there is an old quarter with picturesque alleys located higher up the slopes. And those who venture still higher can enjoy an enchanting panorama. you can sit and enjoy the views in the carefully tended parks. Although Montreux retains a handful of luxury hotels belonging to a past era, its modern hotels, conference and exhibition centre and casino have made it a popular meeting place.

Beautiful 13th-century Chillon Castle is one of the Europe's best-preserved medieval castles. This one-time prison, immortalised by Lord Byron in his poem *The Prisoner of Chillon*, stands on a rock promontory jutting into the lake.

The Château de Chillon, situated on a rocky islet near Montreux

In spring the Golden Rose (Rose d'Or) international television competition and rock festival are big attractions; in July there is a Jazz Festival and in September a Classical Music Festival. Other local festivals and cultural activities help to ensure that there is always something going on in Montreux.

Rue du Théâtre 5
☎ 021 962 8484

65

Montreux Cycle Tour

Distance
17.5km

From the church in the old quarter of Montreux, ride south through Territet on the lakeside road, past the Château de Chillon on the right towards the old town of Villeneuve. About a 0.5km before the centre there is a church on the left. Take the first left after this landmark, left again, then right and pass over the autoroute, following the signs for Col de Chaude. Take the second left, over La Tiniere River and begin a series of increasingly steep switchbacks, which continue for about 3km. Take the first road on the left, signposted Sonchaux and Caux. This continues to climb until the tiny hamlet of Sonchaux is reached, after which it levels out and then descends into the village of Caux. This is the halfway point and is an excellent place to rest a while.

Continue steeply down into Glion, where cyclists wishing to return to Montreux can take the shorter route straight through the village. For those completing the tour, turn right at the village church following the signs for Les Avants. Continue through this beautifully sited resort, taking the mountain road left to the Sonloup Pass. This lies about 1km ahead, after a short climb, and offers marvellous views of the lake and the Savoy Alps. Just after the top station of the railway from Les Avants, turn left for Saumont and then continue down to Chamby. Cross the railway tracks here, and keep them to the left for the ride down to Chernex. Turn left in the village centre for the return to Montreux.

NYON

This a popular summer resort, with a 13th-century castle which flanks Lac Léman. A Celtic settlement, chosen by the Romans as the site for their first garrison town in this part of Helvetia, the former Noviodunum today owes much of its historical face to the influence of the Bernese. The 16th-century castle is their most obvious legacy; it sits squarely above the town with its five-spired towers making a distinctive skyline.

The town's **Musée Romain** features the remains of a 1st-century basilica, discovered in 1974, as well as an extensive collection of artefacts recovered from local excavations. The church of Notre-Dame, dating largely from the 15th century, has some interesting paintings on the north interior wall – pre-dating the main body of the building by an estimated 200 years. Elsewhere in the town, the Place du Marché is notable for its fine-arcaded buildings, again in the Bernese style.

VEVEY

A 'Swiss Riviera' resort with an interesting history arising from its position at the crossroads of Europe since the Roman Empire. Vevey prospered as trade expanded in the Middle Ages and further developed on the arrival of the French Huguenots. Early tourists began to arrive in the 19th century.

The long lakeside promenade is noted for its attractive flowerbeds, and Lac Léman offers a wide range of watersports and cruising opportunities. Every Monday and Saturday the marketplace comes alive with an open market that often includes local wine tastings. Roughly four times a century Vevey celebrates a 'Winegrowers' Festival' (Fête des Vignerons), a huge wine pageant with thousands of people participating. The resort is also a mecca for musicians and filmmakers; it is the venue for the Clara Haskil piano competition and the International Comedy Film Festival; and, along with Montreux, is host to the annual Montreux-Vevey Music Festival.

Together with wine and tourism, chocolate is Vevey's other mainstay. The Nestlé Corporation has its headquarters here and the **Alimèntarium** (Museum of Nutrition) was founded by the company. It covers the natural science, ethnography and history of food. Also of interest is the **Musée Suisse d'Appareils Photographiques** (Swiss Museum of Cameras), a collection of cameras from the late 19th century to the present.

🛈 Avenue Viollier 7
☎ 022 361 6261

Musée Romain
✉ Rue Maupertuis
☎ 022 361 7591
🕐 Apr–Oct: Tue–Sun 10–12, 2–6. Nov–Mar: Tue–Sun 2–6
💷 Cheap

Château de Prangins near Nyon

🛈 Grand Place 29
☎ 021 922 2020

Alimèntarium
✉ Quai Perdonnet
☎ 021 924 4111
🕐 Tue–Sun 10–6
💷 Moderate
🍴 Café

Musée Suisse d'Appareils Photographiques
✉ 4 Grande Place
☎ 021 925 2140
🕐 Mar–Oct: Tue–Sun 11–5:30. Nov–Feb: Tue–Sun 2–5:30
💷 Cheap

67

Ticino

Shaped like an inverted triangle, with its base abutting the broad spine of the main Alpine chain, this 'Italian' corner of Switzerland represents 7 per cent of the country's territory and accommodates just over 4 per cent of its population. Administratively, politically and geographically it is part of the Swiss Confederation, but even the most chauvinistic of Swiss nationals would concede that, culturally, it is defiantly Italian. The predominantly mountainous canton, stretching from the southern flanks of the St Gotthard massif in the north to the Lombardy plain in the south, offers an extraordinary variety of scenery.

Waterfall cascading down the steep sides of Val Bavona, near Foroglio close to the Italian border

ℹ Leventina Turismo, Viale
Stazione
☎ 091 869 1533

*Airolo is the perfect base
for excursions into the
surrounding areas*

AIROLO

Still an all-year resort of some importance, Airolo suffered almost total destruction by fire in 1877. Shortly after rebuilding, the town was almost destroyed again by a massive landslip from the Sasso Rosso – a perpetual menace at the time, now largely obviated by a series of solid embankments. Its most distinctive building is an old church, with a Romanesque belfry, that survived the natural disasters of the last century. In the Gotthardbahn station is a moving memorial to the 277 men who died in the construction of the railway tunnel between 1872 and

1882. Today Airolo is a modest, unremarkable little town elevated from the ordinary by the beauty of its scenery and its convenience as a base for excursions. It also lies at the meeting point of the dramatic Nufenen and St Gotthard passes. Just outside the town a cable car mounts to the 2,065m Sasso della Boggia with fine views northwest.

ℹ Casa Serodine, Viale
Papio
☎ 091 791 0090

ASCONA

Situated in a picturesque bay on Lake Maggiore, Ascona owes its fame to artists. Exhibitions in the cultural Centre and the Museum for Modern Art, countless galleries and antique shops, readings and lectures, bear witness to its active cultural life. Past visitors include Lenin, Jung, Paul Klee and Isadora Duncan.

Giovanni Serodine, arguably the most talented painter from the Ticino, lived here in the 17th century. Three of his

*This cultural centre also
has plenty of outdoor
activities from
windsurfing on Lake
Maggiore to hiking in
the hills*

paintings are hung in the church of Santi Pietro e Paolo. The former sanctuary Collegio Pontificio Papio was endowed in the 16th century by Bartolemeo Papio, a native of Ascona. Its splendid renaissance court is decorated with the heraldry of sponsors and protectors over a period of five centuries. Santa Maria della Misericordia, a church attached to the college, contains valuable frescos.

Castello Grande, the oldest fortress in Bellinzona

Ascona offers a wide range of sports and entertainment from golf and windsurfing to ice-skating and curling. Attractive, well-maintained paths for walking and hiking open up the area round the town, and there is a cycling path from Ascona to Bellinzona (► below), which follows the lake and passes through fields in the Magadino plain. For more than 40 years the annual music festival, held from August to October, has presented classical concerts with world-famous conductors, orchestras and soloists. Another major attraction is the New Orleans Jazz Festival in June and July, when Ascona's squares and alleys take on a particularly lively and colourful atmosphere.

BELLINZONA

The capital city of the Ticino is an important industrial centre and rail transport hub, located halfway between the fruitful Lombard Plain of Italy and the rugged Swiss Alps.

The town has much to fascinate, not least three castles and the ancient city walls. The oldest and largest of the castles is the Castello Grande (or Castle of Uri), first mentioned in documents of the 6th century. The castle's large courtyard was used in times of crisis as a refuge by the entire population. Steep walkways lead from the old city to the castle's heights. The ancient walls have been well-preserved and still link Castello Grande and its counterpart **Castello di Montebello**. This castle originated in the late 13th or early 14th century and was subsequently destroyed and restored on numerous occasions. Its main tower and palazzetto encompass a small museum of both history and archaeology. High above the city is the **Castello di Sasso Corbaro**, built in 1479. Several rooms in its tower are dedicated to a collection of folk art and folklore. The old city below has elegant façades of patrician houses, ornamental iron balconies and gateways, rococo portals and fine inn signs.

🛈 Viale Stazione 18
☎ 091 825 2131

Castello di Montebello Museum
✉ Castello di Montebello
☎ 091 825 13142
🕐 Mar–Nov: Tue–Sun 10–6
💷 Cheap

Castello di Sasso Corbaro
☎ 091 825 5906
🕐 Mar–Nov: Tue–Sun 10–6
💷 Cheap

71

Brissago's tiny subtropical off-shore islands are a popular excursion

ℹ Casa Cavalier Pellanda 4
☎ 091 862 3327

ℹ Via R. Leoncavallo 25
☎ 091 791 0091

Botanical Gardens
☎ 091 791 4361
🕓 Apr–Oct: daily 9–6
🎟 Moderate

BIASCA

A pleasant little town, much like nearby Bellinzona (► 71) in its physical setting, Biasca stands in a narrow basin at the fork of the Valle Leventina and Val Blenio. Mountains rise spectacularly on all sides and the 12th-century church of St Peter and St Paul, cut into the southwestern flank of the 2,329m Pizzo Bagno, is one of the most impressively sited churches in the Ticino. Built in the Romanesque style, it has a tall campanile and contains fascinating 13th-century frescos. The town is the hub of the region's quarrying industry, known for its coarse-grained granite (from which the church is constructed). Biasca is an industrial town, and much of its building is modern but it has appeal, helped by its excellent Ticinese restaurants.

BRISSAGO

This lakeside resort, close to the southwestern frontier with Italy, is visually unremarkable; its austere modern blocks contrast unhappily with fine old Lombardian villas. The village is the lowest spot in Switzerland but the impressive pre-Alpine background helps to compensate for the less than imaginative location of its beautiful location. There is, however, a fine old 16th-century church, protected from the worst excesses of modern architecture by tall cypresses. The best residential villas, high above the busy main road, overlook the two tiny, subtropical Islands of Brissago a few hundred metres offshore. These make a fascinating excursion, and boats from Locarno (► 74) and Ascona (► 70–1) call regularly to visit their **botanical gardens**, home of over 1,500 exotic species.

Nearby, the fine village of Ronco, high above the little port of the same name, has a charming Romanesque church. Erich Maria Remarque, author of *All Quiet on the Western Front*, is buried here.

GANDRIA

The unusual little village of Gandria is a few minutes drive from the eastern border with Italy, on the northern shore of the dark waters of Lake Lugano. Barely signposted, it is easy to miss it and find yourself doing a conspicuous U-turn at the Dogana (customs post). Like many of the best-preserved lakeside villages in the Ticino, the centre is closed to motor vehicles and the car park is situated some way up a narrow lane below the main road. Motorists might be forgiven, therefore, for supposing that visitors are not welcome to this quaint old smuggling haunt. In fact the reverse is true. It is just that most, like the 19th-century smugglers before them, prefer to come by boat, 30 minutes from Lugano (► 74). The hilarious Customs Museum here has information on the interesting (and potentially suicidal) ways people tried to smuggle goods across the Swiss/Italian border. From the wharf the village rises in uneven tiers of colourful, arcaded houses and cafés, with Mount Brè brooding in the background. In the centre of its narrow, flower-decked streets is a charming baroque church, which, in the context of its surroundings, is much-favoured as a subject for paintings and photographs. Gandria has some of the best fish restaurants on Lake Lugano.

The rooftops of the charming village of Gandria, which rises in tiers above the waters of Lake Lugano

Via B, Luini 3
☎ 091 791 0091

Castello Visconti
✉ Piazza Castello
☎ 091 756 3180
🕐 Apr–Oct: Tue–Sun 10–5
💷 Moderate

Above: Locarno's Piazza Grande is the best place in town for pavement coffee and people watching.

LOCARNO

This combination of resort and business centre is on the shores of Lake Maggiore. Along the lakeshore promenade you'll pass subtropical trees, shrubs and flowers. In Locarno's old town patrician houses look simple on the outside yet have magnificent interiors and the old, cosy streets are so narrow you can touch the walls of the opposite houses by stretching your arms. Modern Locarno has department stores, wide avenues and all the up-to-date facilities of a tourist resort.

Locarno's emblem, the pilgrimage church of Madonna del Sasso is reached by funicular from Contrada Cappuccini. The **Castello Visconti** (also known as Rusca) once served as a fortress; today it houses the archaeological museum and its rich collection of local prehistoric and Roman finds. Notable churches include: Sant' Antonio, with magnificent marble altars; Chiesa Nuova, with its stucco ceiling and relics; San Vittore, one of the major Romanesque sacred buildings in the Ticino; and Santa Maria in Selva, which has fine 15th-century frescos. Locarno's International Film Festival held every August is one of the main cultural events in the Ticino.

LUGANO

Lugano is the largest Ticino city and arguably the most beautiful, striking a happy balance between old and new and providing every conceivable amenity at limited cost to its ancient fabric. Because it curves gracefully around the shimmering waters of Lake Lugano and is surrounded by snow-capped mountains on all sides, it has been called the 'Rio de Janeiro of the Old Continent'. Gardens and promenades fringe the lake and there are many pavement cafés to enjoy a cool drink while listening to one of the concerts that are frequently held in the Piazza della

Riformo or the lakeside gardens; Parco Ciani, part of the lakeside promenade, is one of the loveliest parks in Switzerland and is always alive with colour. Take a pedalo out for the best view of the hills that surround the lake.

Lugano has preserved its fascinating traffic-free historic centre and has two of the most famous churches in Ticino: San Lorenzo and St Mary of the Angels. The latter has masterly fresco's by Bernadino Luini, one of Leonardo da Vinci's best students. Lugano offers a wide choice of bars, restaurants and sophisticated nightspots. Alternatively, a quiet stroll along the waterfront or an evening cruise may appeal. The Lake Festival is held at the end of July and the Vintage Parade, on the first Sunday in October, draw the whole town together for a good time.

MALCANTONE

This is a rugged, beautiful and heavily wooded district famed for its unspoiled villages – many of which are set in ascending terraces on the southern flanks of Monte Lema and connected by a labyrinth of winding country lanes. From Cademario there are excellent views of the lake and the Ticino Alps, and the added bonus of the charming 12th-century church of San Ambrogio. Inside the church are some interesting murals painted between the 13th and 15th centuries. There is another fine church in the village of Miglieglia, a few miles further west. Built in the 15th century, Santo Stefano Al Colle contains some equally impressive late Gothic frescos. Miglieglia is also the station for the cable car up to the summit of Monte Lema. From the restaurant at the top station it is a 10-minute up a steep path to the highest viewing point from where there are marvellous views.

ℹ Piazza Lago
☎ 091 606 2986

Cruising on Lake Lugano

ℹ Via Angelo Maspoli 15
☎ 091 646 5761

Museo d'Arte
✉ Piazza S Giovanni
☎ 091 646 7649
🕐 Tue–Sun 10–12, 2–5
👍 Cheap

Vincenzo Vela Museum
✉ Largo Vincenzo Vela
☎ 091 640 7044
🕐 Mar–May, Oct to
   mid–Nov: Tue–Sun 10–5
👍 CHF5
🍴 Café

MENDRÍSIO

Mendrísio is the district capital and lies at the heart of a network of attractive villages in the southernmost part of the Ticino. The district feels more Italian than Swiss, with a strong Lombardian inheritance and a reputation for some of the finest wines in the country. This is a predominantly rural area, although Mendrísio is hardly a sleepy backwater. It is a charming, lively place celebrated for its festivals and processions. Over the Easter period the streets are richly decorated with flowers and banners, and a series of colourful depictions of the main events leading up to the Crucifixion take place. The torchlight procession on Good Friday is an arresting sight.

The main church of St Cosima and St Damian is one of the town's most imposing buildings, but there are several earlier structures including the stately 16th-century Palazzo Torriani-Fontana and the Palazzo Pollini (1720) now the **Museo d'Arte**. Almost 4km west the village of Lignoretto has the **Vincenzo Vela Museum** in the former home of this renowned sculptor.

MONTE GENEROSO

Reached from Lugano via the pleasant village of Bissone, Monte Generoso offers one of the great Alpine panoramas. A perfect vantage point for views over the Lombardy plain, the Italian and Swiss lakes, and the distant Bernese and Valais Alps, it is reached after a 40-minute trip by cogwheel railway from the small village of Capolago opposite Riva San Vitale. At 1,701m, it is the highest mountain in the region, and is famed for its rich variety of flora. The meadows are great for Alpine flowers such as gentian. Beneath the crest, on its southwestern flank, is a beautiful Alpine garden in the hamlet of Bella Vista – reached by road 7.5km northeast of Mendrísio (▶ above). There are magnificent views from here as well.

MORCOTE

This is unquestionably the most picturesque of the lakeside villages in the area known as the Ceresio. Palms, promenades, cypresses, ornate lamps and arcaded villas create a colourful mosaic in this former fishing village – now an artists' colony. The predominant colour here is terracotta. A short climb up cobbled alleys leads to the 14th-century church of the Madonna of the Rock with its tall, distinctive campanile. Inside, there are fine 16th-century frescos and an impressive 17th-century organ.

Just outside Morcote, Parco Scherrer is another example of the beautiful landscaped gardens in the area. It contains a rich variety of subtropical trees and plants, and some splendid classical buildings. North of the village (4km) is the equally exclusive resort of Figino, notable for its extravagant villas overlooking Lake Lugano into Italy.

Between Morcote and Lugano at Melide is Swissminiatur with scale models of all the main Swiss sights, including operating cable cars and railways. Tour Switzerland in an afternoon.

A waterfront street lined with Lombardic arcaded buildings, in the village of Morcote

TICINO VALLEYS

The Ticino is renowned for its beautiful valleys, ranking in scenic attraction with the best of the Swiss landscape.

Plunging dramatically from the Valle Santa Maria beneath the Lukmanierpass, Val Blenio is one of the most beautiful of all Swiss valleys. At regular intervals along its twisting path are enchanting mountain villages, characterised by their sunny setting and their diminutive size.

Running southeast from the Ticino end of the St Gotthard Pass, the Valle Leventina has the largest 'vertical drop' of any traversible valley in Europe (974m). It is surprisingly unaffected by the N2 autobahn, which follows its path. Far from blighting the area, the fast road has proved to be a boon in relieving the old valley highway of its former congestion. Many of the towns and villages along the valley floor have recaptured some tranquillity. The most appealing stretch of the valley lies between the villages of Quinto and Giornico, bisected by the river and linked by a quaint old arched bridge.

Climbing northwards from Locarno (► 74), the Valle Maggia is famous for its *rusticis* – former peasant dwellings two or three centuries old. Cevio, historically the administrative centre of the valley, is the point of access to

The distinctive stone statues and buildings of Valle Maggia, Cevio

*The small village of
Sonlerto with its
characteristic local style
of building and beautiful
little churches*

a network of enchanting valleys fanning out in all directions. The road west leads up the spectacular Valle di Campo, and north of that the Valle di Bosco/Gurin. Wandfluhhorn Pizzo Biela is the highest in the Ticino at 1,505m. Immediately to the north of Cevio is the delightful Bignasco, and here the Maggia splits into another two valleys – the Val Bavona and the Val Lavizzara. The former, a densely wooded gorge of considerable beauty, leads to the remote hamlet of San Carlo beneath the peak of Basódino and its impressive glacier. A chair lift leads up to a cluster of mountain lakes.

West of the Valle Centovalli (the 'hundred valleys'), itself an area of considerable beauty, the Valle Onsernone is entered from the village of Cavigliano (7km out of Locarno). Smaller than many of the neighbouring Ticino valleys, it follows a serpentine course up through the charming villages of Loco, Russo and Crana. It ends at Spruga, where a bridlepath leads over the mountainous frontier into Italy. The valley is one of the most fascinating in the canton, characterised by overhanging precipices and plunging ravines.

Val Verzasca is the most remote of the larger Ticino valleys – a veritable wilderness of dramatic defiles, river gorges and breathtaking scenery. It runs 25km north of Gordola on Locarno's eastern perimeter, and ends after a steep and beautiful climb to the mountain village of Sonogno. Two-thirds of the way up at the river fork is Brione, the principal village of the valley.

Valais & Vaud

Within this southwest part of the country, you will find yourself juggling with the contrasting images of medieval towns surrounded by sun-baked terraced vineyards, and the awesome might of the highest peaks and longest glaciers in the country. This is the region of remote and wild valleys, mountain hamlets apparently untouched by time, scorched-wood centuries-old chalets, sun-bleached scree slopes, crystal-clear mountain lakes and stunning Alpine scenery. It is also the region that offers the widest choice of mountain resorts, ranging from the world's most sophisticated to the pleasingly unpretentious. But if there is one image that captures this region's essence, it is perhaps the distinctive jagged outline of the 4,478m Matterhorn.

Flowers and wooden houses in the small town of Evolene in the fertile Val d'Herens

Rue Columb 5
☎ 024 466 3030

**Musée de la Vigne et du
Vin/Musée de l'Etiquette**
✉ Château d'Aigle
☎ 024 466 2130
🕐 Apr–Oct: Tue–Sun
10–12:30, 2–6 (Jul, Aug
10–6)
♿ Moderate

AIGLE

An attractive little town on the banks of the turbulent
Grand Eau in the Rhône Valley. Formerly a feudal
stronghold of importance, it was ruled by the House of
Savoy before being taken by Bern (► 36) in the 15th
century, and it remained under Bernese control until the
French invasion of 1798. The French influence is still
predominant. The town is known chiefly for its wine-
making heritage and its imposing 13th-century château,
surrounded by vineyards. Rebuilt by the Bernese in the
15th century, the Château d'Aigle is one of the most
important fortress sites in Switzerland. Comprising a
square keep and three round towers, it now houses two
museums, **Musée de la Vigne et du Vin** devoted to wine,
the other **Musée de l'Etiquette** to salt. A huge 17th-
century barn adjoins the château. In Cloitre, the town's
oldest quarter, the church of St Maurice founded in the
12th century is notable for its late-Gothic steeple.

In the Fontaine quarter, the Rue de Jérusalem is a
charming alley of old arcaded houses. Other attractions
include the old market square, the pedestrianised Rue du
Bourg, and the medieval church of St Jacques with a
tower dating from 1642.

*The 12th century Château
d'Aigle, framed by
vineyards*

Aigle Car Tour

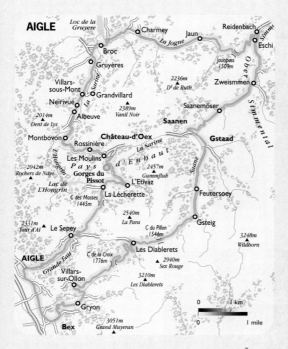

AIGLE

Loc de la Gruyere · Charmey · Jaun · Reidenbach · Eschi
La Jogne · Jaunpass 1509m · Ober · Simm
Broc · Gruyères · Zweismmen
Villars-sous-Mont · Grandvillard · 2236m D^t de Ruth · Saanemöser
Neirivue · La Sarine · 2389m Vanil Noir · **Saanen**
2014m Dent de Lys · Albeuve · **Gstaad**
Montbovon · Rossinière · **Château-d'Oex** · La Sarine · d'Enhaut · Saane
Les Moulins · Pays · 2457m Gummfluh
2042m Rochers de Naye · L'Hongrin · Gorges du Pissot · L'Etivaz
Lac de L'Hongrin · C des Mosses 1445m · La Lécherette · Feutersoey
2540m La Para · C du Pillon 1546m · Gsteig · 3248m Wildhorn
2331m Tour d'Ai · Le Sepey
AIGLE · C de la Croix 1776m · Les Diablerets · 2940m Sex Rouge
Grande Eau · Villars-sur-Ollon · 3210m Les Diablerets
Gryon
Bex · 3051m Grand Muveran

0 — 1 km
0 — 1 mile

From Aigle go northeast on Route 11, signed Leysin and Château-d'Oex, taking the steep road on the left bank of Grande Eau to Les Planches. Continue to Col des Mosses and descend to Château-d'Oex. From the centre, take the road to Rossinière and Gruyères and head into Montbovon. After 7km right turn to Grandvillard, continuing north to medieval Gruyères. Turn right after the town, passing through Broc towards Charmey on the Jaun Pass road. The main pass road climbs through Jogne Gorge to Jaun. Pass through dramatic corniche sections for the 1,509m Jaunpass, with spectacular views. The road winds steeply down to Reidenbach where you rejoin Route 11, heading south up Ober Simmental to Zweisimmen. Continue on to Saanen, turning left and south for Gstaad, then head south to Gsteig ascending to Col du Pillon beneath the peaks of Les Diablerets and to the resort of the same name, 4km ahead. Go south over the Col de La Croix to Villars-sur-Ollon, passing through the resort; turn left for Gryon and Bex. The steep descent to Route 9 heads north to Aigle.

Distance
35km

ℹ Bahnhofplatz
☎ 027 921 6030

BRIG

This lively historic town is a key road and rail junction in the Valais and because of its position at the head of the Simplon Pass, it has traditionally provided a trade route

with Italy. It also stands at the mouth of the famous Simplon rail tunnel, built between 1898 and 1904, which at 19.8km is one of the world's longest. Perhaps because of this geographical location, Brig has earned an unhelpful reputation as a place to pass through. However, that does a considerable disservice to the town and its attractions.

The formidable Stockalperschloss (Stockalper's Palace), built between 1658 and 1678, is said to be the finest of Switzerland's baroque palaces, and its three striking, onion-domed gilded towers give an early impression of the town's architectural treasures. These comprise several other fine buildings, including an old Jesuit church (built in 1662), and a collection of elegant mansions built on the profits of cross-border trade with Italy. The fountain in the Marktplatz commemorates one of aviation's unsung pioneers, Georges Chavez – he was the first man to fly

Flags flying in Brig

over the Alps, from Brig to the Italian town of Domodossola in 1910, but he was killed on landing.

ℹ Avenue de la Gare
☎ 026 912 8022

Musée Gruérien
✉ Rue de la Condémine 25
☎ 026 912 7260
🕐 Tue–Sat 10–12, 2–5; Sun 2-5
💶 Cheap

BULLE

Lying in the heart of Gruyère, the small town of Bulle is best known for its cheeses named after the region. This delightful pastoral area in the northwest foothills of the Alps is considered one of the prettiest parts of Switzerland. It has managed to retain much of its rustic flavour and has numerous cheese shops lining its main street. Its unusual underground museum, the **Musée Gruérien**, has a cheese room faithfully reconstructed from part of a herdsman's mountain lodge. The town has an imposing 13th-century castle and near by is a 14th-century Capuchin chapel, formerly part of a long-vanished hospital. Rebuilt in 1454 after a fire, its splendid carved wooden doors and baroque high altar date from 1662.

CHAMPÉRY

Facing the jagged peaks of the Dents du Midi, Champéry is a sleepy Alpine sports resort in a spectacular setting. Linked to the largest skiing region in the world – the resorts of the Portes du Soleil – it is popular with those skiers who prefer more Alpine charm than the neighbouring French resorts provide. Most of the main street is closed to traffic and the best of the restaurants and shops are found on its gentle descent to the main cable car station to Planachaux. One of its most attractive buildings is an early 18th-century church, with an intriguing old lantern capping its baroque bell tower.

The majority of the resort's newer development is concentrated around the valley road curving beneath the heart of the old village, which has managed to retain much of its traditional flavour. As befits an all-year resort, Champéry offers a full range of facilities.

CHAMPEX

One of the most delightful spots in the Valais, Champex is a charming all-year resort on the edge of a miniature lake. Close to the border with France, it stands at the mouth of the densely wooded Val Ferret sheltered by the Mont Blanc massif to the west and the Grand Combin to the east.

Lac du Champex is so evenly contoured you might be forgiven for assuming that it is man-made, and its glass-like surface lends further substance to that impression. In the summer the lake offers swimming and boating; in winter it becomes a natural ice-rink.

On its northern shore the resort's only road curves around the water's edge, lined by elegant Victorian hotels and somewhat newer restaurants and cafés. Across the lake stands a tiny, 19th-century Protestant chapel, illuminated at night and reached by a pretty path through fir trees.

Residence Opaline
☎ 024 479 2020

Above: *looking through bushes across the tiny mirror of a lake to the resort of Champex surrounded by forested peaks*

Village centre, on the main street
☎ 027 783 1227

La Place
☎ 026 924 2525

Musée du Vieux Pays d'Enhaut
✉ On the main road
☎ 026 924 6520
🕐 Tue–Sun 2–5. Closed Nov
💰 Cheap

CHÂTEAU-D'OEX

A traditional mountain village with chalet-style houses, and a growing winter-sports resort. The ski runs offer various levels of skill and are accessible by drag lifts, cable cars and chair lifts. There are also numerous walking trails through pine forests and meadows.

A visit to the Nature Reserve of La Pierreuse to see the chamois is popular, while the most spectacular cable-car ride is that from Diablerets village – accessible by train and postbus – to a glacier with superb views. Visitors can go white-river rafting on the River Sarine – from May to mid-August – or fishing for trout in the Sarine or nearby lakes such as Rossinière and L'Hongrin. The resort offers a variety of other activities from tennis to hot-air ballooning (a famous hot-air balloon festival is held every January).

Tourism is the mainstay of this valley but agriculture and craftsmanship play an important role, reflected in the **Musée du Vieux Pays d'Enhaut** (Enhaut Traditional Museum), with a fine collection of engravings, paper silhouettes and stained glass windows.

Avenue de la Gare
☎ 027 485 0404

Golfers make their way to the next fairway, overshadowed by mountains and forested slopes in Crans-Montana

CRANS-MONTANA

Before World War I the adjoining villages of Crans and Montana were two separate resorts. In some respects they still are, with Crans strong on city chic and designer boutiques, and the lower village of Montana noticeably more parochial. The 'merger' has made this one of the largest sports resorts in Switzerland.

Frequently described as a 'suburban sprawl', the extraordinary beauty of Montana's 'balcony' setting makes any criticism seem almost churlish. Admittedly, the architecture is at best undistinguished and the traffic-choked roads leave something to be desired, but this is an unashamed 'super-resort' geared to the comfort and convenience of its largely affluent clientele. Because of its extensive range of facilities it has become a popular place to buy a second home for many Swiss.

In the summer you can swim in the many small lakes that surround the Crans part of the resort, and the walking possibilities are extensive.

Cable car to the skiing
areas of Les Diablerets

Summer skiing is available on the sinister-sounding Plaine
Morte glacier. In winter the resort is served by 150km of
piste and, although by comparison with other Valais
resorts the skiing is fairly low, it is undeniably pretty, split
evenly between open and wooded terrain. From either
Crans or Montana base stations, the ascent by gondola
and then cable car to Bella Lui at 2,543m offers one of the
great Alpine panoramas over the Rhône Valley.

LES DIABLERETS

The holiday resort of Les Diablerets is situated some
1,200m above sea-level in the very heart of the Vaudoise
Alps at the foot of a mountain range capped by a
breathtaking glacier. Parallel development of agriculture
and tourism is one of the characteristics of this mountain
village, which dates from the Middle Ages, and which
today offers a wide choice of accommodation in hotels,
rented apartments and chalets.

    In summer Les Diablerets is the starting point for many
walks or hikes across an extensive nature reserve, with a
wide network of marked paths. An excursion to the
Diablerets glacier is a special experience. It takes an aerial
cable car only 35 minutes to reach the glacier at 3,000m
above sea-level, where the snow never melts and where
visitors can often enjoy summer skiing or set off for walks
and mountain tours. There are also guided trips on a
snowbus across the glacier.

Rue de la Gare
☎ 024 492 3358

The ancient Pont Berne, built entirely of wood with a shingle roof, crossing the Sarine River in Fribourg

---

i Avenue de la Gare
☎ 026 321 3175

Musée d'Art et d'Histoire
✉ Rue de Morat 12
☎ 026 305 5140
🕐 Tue–Sun 11–6 (Thu 11–8)
♿ Cheap

DID YOU KNOW?

Although this medieval town nestles next to the Vaud region, it is actually the capital of its own canton, Fribourg, established in the 15th century.

FRIBOURG

The heart of Fribourg's old town unfolds in all its medieval splendour with narrow curved streets and stairways flanked by Gothic façades. In the Bourg quarter, magnificently preserved and restored period houses cluster about the Cathédral Saint-Nicholas. The elegant pavement cafés on Rue de Romont and Rue de Lausanne make for a welcome pause to rest and people watch. Witness to six centuries of history, the collegiate church, which became a cathedral when Fribourg was elevated to a bishopric, contains masterpieces in stained glass as well as a renowned organ built by Aloys Mooser.

The **Musée d'Art et d'Histoire** (Museum of Art and History) is one of the most visited in Switzerland. In addition to numerous expositions of excellent classical and modern art, it contains manifold collections covering local and national history and art, from prehistoric times to the present day. Its extension into the house known as the 'Abbattoir' (a one-time slaughterhouse) enables visitors to admire major sculptures from the Middle Ages.

Looking down the Goms Valley from the Furka Pass, which leads from Oberwald down into central Switzerland

GOMS VALLEY

Also known as the Conches Valley, or Upper Rhône Valley, Goms is the name given to this upper region of the Valais by its predominantly German-speaking inhabitants. The lateral road climbs steadily west to east along the north bank of the river for 48km from Brig (➤ 84) to the high-lying glacier town of Gletsch. Scenery of ever-increasing grandeur unfolds at every stage of this climb, and each new village, at regular intervals along the route, appears to surpass its lower neighbour in charm and character.

🛈 Tourismusbüro, 3984
Fiesch
☎ 027 970 1070

MARTIGNY

A small industrial town of modest charm at the point where the Rhône takes a sharp right turn up towards Lac Léman. It is also the place where the routes from the Grand St-Bernard, Forclaz and Simplon passes converge. The modern town is an excellent starting point for excursions – the French and Italian borders are well within an hour's drive, and major international skiing resorts such as Verbier (➤ 91), Crans-Montana (➤ 86–7) and Champéry (➤ 85) are similarly accessible.

In recent years Martigny has experienced something of a Roman renaissance, which has given it new pride in its cultural inheritance. In 1976 a 1st-century Roman temple was excavated near the Rue du Forum, and two years later the **Musée Gallo-Roman** was constructed over the foundations. This impressive building has a range of galleries overlooking the site of the temple and it contains a comprehensive collection of Roman artefacts. It also includes a veteran car collection of more than 40 vehicles dating from 1897. A short distance away, across the Route du Levant, is a late 1st-century Roman amphitheatre that once held up to 6,000 spectators.

Château de la Bâtiaz, an imposing, ruined medieval castle built in 1259, stands high over the town on a rocky bluff, and offers delightful views of the Martigny basin and its vineyards. The 19th-century town hall in Place Centrale is an ambitious architectural enterprise for its time that is justly celebrated for its remarkable 54.8sq m stained-glass window illustrating the Rhône and Dranse rivers.

🛈 Place Centrale 9
☎ 027 721 2220

Musée Gallo-Roman & de l'Automobile
✉ Fondation Pierre Gianadda, Rue du Forum 59
☎ 027 722 3978
🕐 Nov–Jun: daily 10–6; Jun–Nov 9–7
✋ Expensive
🍴 Café

MÜNSTER

The principal village of the Goms Valley, attractively placed at the foot of the rugged Minstigertal Valley plunging steeply from the high Aargrat ridge on the Valais/Bernese Oberland border. Münster centre is split by the main valley road, which runs alongside the north bank of the Rhône. The village is particularly notable for its fine 15th- and 16th-century blackwood chalets and traditional storehouses raised on stone mushroom-shaped staddle stones. The parish church of St Mary, founded in the 13th century, retains a Romanesque belfry from the same period. The interior has a number of interesting features, including an ornate, Gothic high altar of 1509. Above the village, on the western side of the Minstigertal, is the small chapel of St Anthony of Padua, built in 1680 and altered a century later.

SAAS FEE

ℹ️ First building on right as you enter the village
☎ 027 958 1858

The charming village of Saas Fee lies among magnificent mountains and glaciers in the heart of the highest Swiss Alps. No cars are allowed in the village centre, but transport is provided by horse-drawn sleigh or small electrically powered vehicles. The village has retained its Alpine flavour – weather-beaten chalets and clusters of ancient barns are protected by the community, but some have been modernised to offer comfortable accommodation and shops. The 'Pearl of the Alps', as Saas Fee is known, is

The Eispavillon inside the glacier at Saas Fee

A climber near Saas Fee with a mountain guide

surrounded by 13 mountains including the multi-summited Monte Rosa, Europe's second highest peak. For winter skiers, it is one of the best resorts in Switzerland. The 'Metro Alpin' (installed in 1984) is the world's highest underground funicular, running from Felskinn to Mittelallin. It takes skiers up to 3,500m where, of course, snow is always guaranteed. Summer mountaineering is also a prime activity at the resort.

VERBIER

Verbier, dominated by the 3,000m-high Mont Gelé, is an exceptionally well-equipped resort. Haphazard building and planning do not make it attractive, but it offers superb skiing, making it one of the country's most popular wintersports resorts, especially with the younger crowd. There is a vast network of lifts, cable cars and ski runs, with slopes for every kind of skier, together with a good range of facilities. Mont Gelé is reached by three cable cars; from the cross that indicates you are at the rocky summit of Mont Gelé there are marvellous views of the Mont Blanc and Grand Combin massifs.

 Place Centrale
☎ 027 775 3888

ℹ️ Rue Centrale
☎ 024 495 3232

VILLARS

At 1,300m above sea-level on a plateau high above the Rhône Valley, and commanding a superb panoramic view of the Vaudois Alps, the Valaisan Alps and Mont Blanc, Villars is one of Switzerland's premier winter resorts – and one of the best equipped.

In winter the resort offers 120km of prepared pistes, ranging from gentle nursery slopes to the 3,000m high glacier at Les Diablerets (▶ 87), linked to the Villars ski region. In summer, too, there is plenty to entertain: 300km

of delightful mountain walks along the many well-marked footpaths, or get a view of the whole Alpine chain by taking an aerial cable car to the Roc d'Orsay at 2,000m. The modern leisure club offers everything from squash and volleyball to a Turkish bath, and even has an electronically controlled 18-hole golf course simulator. Other facilities include swimming pools, an ice-skating rink and a real golf course, and there are opportunities for parachuting and fishing in the mountain lakes.

Excellent footpaths take walkers into the mountains in summer

ℹ️ Bahnhofplatz 5
☎ 027 966 8111

Alpine Museum
✉ Postfach 285
☎ 027 967 4100
🕐 Jun–Oct: daily 10–12, 4–6. Jul & Aug: 10–12, 3–6. rest of year 4:30–6:30 (closed Sat)
💰 Moderate

ZERMATT

Surrounded by some of Europe's highest mountains, Zermatt is an excellent ski resort, with near perfect skiing at an altitude that makes the snow conditions more reliable than at other resorts. Zermatt caters for all grades and has extensive uphill transport, ample mountain restaurants, and over 160km of prepared pistes. The cable car takes you up to the Little Matterhorn, the highest ski station in Europe, with views over the mountain range.

The village can only be reached by railway and in the summer you might catch sight of marmots scampering away as the train passes. There is no motor traffic and the resort centre is beautifully maintained in traditional style, although cowsheds have given way to Rolex and Gucci shops and five-star hotels. It also boasts its own art gallery, the Galerie Matterhorn, and the **Alpine Museum**, which contains relics of the first conquests of the Matterhorn.

Zermatt's summer visitors come to walk on the Matterhorn's slopes and to see the wealth of wild flowers on the high pastures. It is possible to walk the Gornergrat rack railway, one of Europe's highest cogwheel railways, up to the Riffelberg, from where you have an excellent view of the Matterhorn (actually best viewed from here), and then walk down to Zermatt via Ritti and Winkelmatten.

Zermatt Mountain Walk

Take the funicular, east of Zermatt's main steet, to the station at Riffelalp then take the cliff path east towards the Findelgletscher, signposted Grüensee (the 'green lake') – a pleasant, level walk through larch and pine woods.

After about 1km there is a fork. Continue to the right along the upper path that begins to climb gradually towards the lake. Pass the restaurant and skirt the northern bank of the lake (which is popular with swimmers). The trail carries on, over a couple of streams, to a point where it merges with a lower path that leads over another stream by the side of a tiny lake on the right.

Continue to the delightful and relatively quiet Grindjisee, concealed in a fold between the mountainside and the glacial moraine. The waterfall above the lake feeds a sparkling brook. This is a fine picnic spot, with views of the Matterhorn to the southwest and the Findelgletscher rolling down the flank of the Stockhorn to the east. Return to the path and after a short distance take a right fork past the milky-coloured Mosjesee lake on the left. It then descends to Findeln hamlet, with wooden barns and houses.

From here, follow signs for Winkelmatten descending on broad switchbacks through woods to the tracks of the cog railway. Cross these, and follow the path round to the left through the centre of Winkelmatten. The path then descends to the bottom of the Furri gondola where it joins the road back into Zermatt.

Distance
13km
Time
Allow 3 hours

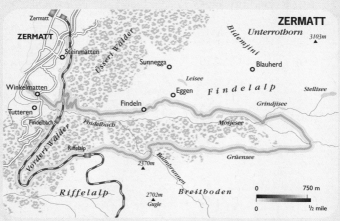

Grisons

The largest of Switzerland's cantons, covering about a sixth of the country's landmass, the Grisons (also known by its German name of 'Graubünden') is the only one where three languages – German, Italian and Romansch – are spoken. It comprises remote farms and villages and numerous popular holiday resorts such as glitzy St Moritz, Davos, Flims and Klosters. It is also the most sparsely populated, with about 24 inhabitants per square kilometre, compared to a Swiss average of 150. Almost exclusively Alpine in character, the canton is the only one in the country that completely straddles the Alps.

Paragliders catch the wind at Davos in the Grisons

Davos
Mountain Walk

Distance
14km
Time
Allow 3 hours

*The funicular from
Davos Dorf*

Take the two-stage funicular from Davos Dorf to the Weissfluhjoch, and exit from the rear of the top station. Make a short, steep descent to the foot of the Weissfluh. Turn right, following the signs to the Parsennhütte and keeping the Schifer gondola overhead to the right hand side. After a short distance a couple of paths drop to the tiny lake under the Totalphorn on the right. Ignore these and continue ahead for about another 15 minutes.

Just past the Schwarzhorn a fork in the path is signposted Schifer to the left and Parsennhütte to the right. Take the latter and make the brief ascent under the gondola to the top of a short draglift on the Parsennfurgga. It's a steep but scenic descent to the Parsennhütte and adjacent lift station. This is a pleasant place to stop for refreshments

The famous Parsenn snowfields are a short stroll behind the restaurant, but the return to Davos is via the panoramic Höhenweg through the small tunnel directly in front of the Parsennhütte, and taking the left path. This winds briefly past a drag-lift on the right, and then climbs gently beneath the Totalphorn. The views into Davos are dramatic. The path then crosses another draglift for a choice of routes, either to the Höhenweg station or down a steep and pretty descent through woods into Meierhof above the lake. It is then a 15-minute walk back to the starting point.

🛈 Poststrasse (close to the
casino)
☎ 081 378 7020

*Easy hiking over Davos's
streams for all age-groups*

AROSA
This long-established and popular resort is an attractive and lively village remotely set in superb scenery at the head of the spectacular Plessur Valley. Arosa combines much of the sophistication of St Moritz (► 99) with the casual, relaxed atmosphere of many smaller Swiss resorts.

For winter-sports enthusiasts there are varied slopes and all the ski areas are interconnecting, forming a well-planned and efficient network with over 72km of downhill runs that are prepared and patrolled. Langlauf (cross-country skiing) is popular, and there are nearly 32km of special pistes. Other facilities include a toboggan run, two natural ice-skating rinks and two artificial rinks, bowling alleys and a casino.

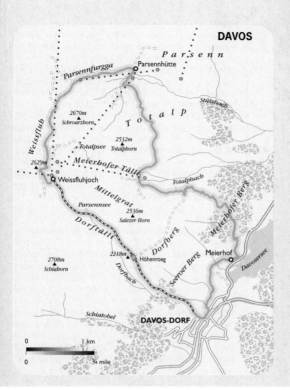

DAVOS

Map labels:
Parsenn, Parsennhütte, Parsennfurgga, Stützbach, 2670m Schroarzborn, Totalp, 2532m Totalpborn, Weissflub, Totalpsee, Meierbofer Tälli, 2629m, Totalpbach, Weissfluhjoch, Mittelgrat, Meierbofer Berg, Parsennsee, 2536m Salezer Horn, Dorftälli, Dorfberg, Meierhof, 2708m Schiaborn, 2218m Höhenroeg, Dorfbach, Seetorer Berg, Davosersee, Schiatobel, **DAVOS-DORF**

0   1 km
0   ¾ mile

DAVOS

The largest ski resort of the Grisons, Davos provides some of the world's best skiing, with a fine lift system, reliable snow conditions and a host of après-ski facilities.

Located in a peaceful Alpine valley, it is divided into two parts – Platz and Dorf – and is lively, if architecturally undistinguished, with a number of charming restaurants, cafés and stylish boutiques. It has a long history as a health resort, and was famously patronised by Robert Louis Stevenson and Sir Arthur Conan-Doyle.

The ski slopes that attract the crowds are on the sides of the Strela chain of mountains, dominated by the Weissfluhjoch (nearly 2,750m high). Here are the most remarkable snowfields in the country, which can be reached via the Parsenn funicular railway. In summer Davos is equally delightful. It has more than 450km of well-kept walks and paths through town, mountains and forest. Climbing and mountaineering is organised and the resort also offers watersports on the Lake of Davos, trout fishing and an 18-hole golf course.

 Promenade 67, Davos Platz
☎ 081 415 2121

🖈 Flims Waldhaus
☎ 081 920 9202

FLIMS

The people of Flims still speak the local Romansch dialect, apparently indifferent to the colourful mix of tongues brought by the international skiing set. Set on a terrace above the Rhein gorge amid spectacular scenery, it is still essentially a village – in fact two villages: Flims-Dorf, the traditional residential section and Flims-Waldhaus, whose hotels are scattered through a forest of conifers.

The resort enjoyed modest fame in the late 19th century as a spa, attracting a number of illustrious guests including members of the Dutch royal family. It really took off, however, after World War II, when Europe's first chair lift was installed between the village and Foppa. In 1956 the 2,675m peak of Cassons Grat was connected by cable car from Naraus, and Flims' reputation as one of the country's leading ski resorts was assured.

🖈 Alte Bahnhofstrasse
☎ 081 410 2020

KLOSTERS

Three decades of popularity with royalty, film stars and the jet-set have not spoiled Klosters. Nestled beneath a sparkle of snow-covered peaks, this fairytale village comes complete with horse-drawn sleighs, friendly locals and a cluster of picturesque chalets. Skiers have the choice of 24 mountain railways and ski lifts, all within a stone's throw of the village. Of the numerous ski runs in the Gotschna/Parsenn area, the favourite is still the descent from the top of the Weissfluh down to Küblis. Cross-country skiers have for many years sung the praises of Klosters. Nor are walkers forgotten with a choice of well-prepared, clearly marked paths ranging from gentle walks near the village to more challenging itineraries. And for those who prefer a 'holiday on ice', Klosters also offers curling and skating on the two natural rinks.

Klosters lies in the Prättigau valley alongside the Landquart River

PONTRESINA

A small village resort with buildings in the typical Engadine painted style, which lies in a sheltered valley and shares the same ski area as St Moritz (▶ below). It is much less sophisticated than St Moritz, but is charming nevertheless – and much cheaper and friendlier than its neighbour!

Along the narrow streets some of the elegant Edwardian hotels would not look out of place in the most prestigious of the world's resorts. Close to the main road beneath the village of Punt Muragel a funicular station leads to the peak of Muottas Muragel. The summit provides a superb view of the Engadine Valley and the Bernina massif.

🛈 Kongresszentrum Rondo
☎ 081 838 8300

Engadine's 450km of hiking paths pass through wonderful scenery

ST MORITZ

Located on the southern side of the Alps at an altitude of 1,856m above sea-level, this remains one of Switzerland's best-known and best-loved resorts. St Moritz's first visitors came for the healing mineral springs that were discovered as long ago as the Bronze Age. St Moritz-Dorf lies halfway up the slope at the foot of the leaning campanile (Schiefer Turm), the only vestige of the original village, and is bristling with palatial hotels. St Moritz Bad is the spa quarter, its extensive installations spreading around the lake.

🛈 Via Maistra 12
☎ 081 837 3333

The town is the birthplace of winter tourism and modern winter sports in the Alps, and is Switzerland's only Olympic host resort. The high probability of snow and good weather, thanks to the high altitude and southern exposure, ensures a long winter season, with visitors attracted by the possibilities for downhill and cross-country skiing and other attractions such as the Cresta bob run. In summer, the chief appeal of St Moritz lies in the wide range of sports activities available, such as summer skiing, watersports, ice-skating and golf on the highest and oldest 18-hole golf course in Continental Europe.

Samedan, backed by the forest-clad lowers slopes of the Bernina, which rise up to snow-capped summits above

SAMEDAN

A charming, typically Engadine Village, Samedan found international fame as a haven for golfers in the early part of the 20th century. Its 18-hole golf course is still one of the most enduring attractions in the game. Set back off the north side of the new road between Zuoz (➤ 103) and St Moritz (➤ 99), the resort occupies a delightful site at the foot of the Bernina Valley facing the Bernina massif. The church in the centre is 18th-century, and on the western side of the village is another, late-Gothic church containing the family vault of the Plantas. This was an influential Engadine family whose imposing former residence is now a centre of Romansch culture. Situated on the road east out of the village towards the small hamlet of Bever, the Chesa Planta is one of the finest examples of Engadine architecture in the region.

Samedan Car Tour

From Samedan follow Route 27 northeast leaving the main road to enter the picturesque town of Zuoz. Rejoin the main road along the left bank of the En River to Zernez. Continue to the village of Susch, turning left here up the winding mountain road to the Flüelapass, threading through the rocky Val Susasca. The road descends through the barren landscape of the Flüela to the bustling resort of Davos. Drive southwest along its main street, following the signs for Tiefencastel then pass through the ancient hamlet of Frauenkirch. Threading a series of tunnels in the Zügen defile, the road enters the Landwasser Gorge before meeting the Albulapass road just before Tiefencastel. Follow Route 3 for the Julierpass and St Moritz. Continue south to Savognin. From here the road continues through the Tinizong village and climbs through Rona and Bivio and on to the Julierpass. The road now descends sharply to the old resort of Silvaplana, where it joins Route 27 northeast along the north bank of Lake Silvaplana to St Moritz, and from here skirting the lake of St Moritz (L. de San Murexxan) back to Samedan.

Distance
Approximately 128.5km

i Hauptstrasse (near the
post office)
☎ 081 861 2222

Chagronda Museum
✉ Plaz
🕐 Jul–Sep: Mon, Tue, Wed,
Fri 3–6. Mid-May to end
Jun and Oct: Tue and Thu
4–6. Mid-Dec to Easter:
Tue and Thu guided tours
only at 5PM
🎟 Cheap

i Neudorfstrasse 49
☎ 081 651 1134

SCUOL

The cultural centre of the Lower Engadine and the last
town of any size before the Austro-Swiss border, Scuol is
a major spa complex comprising the two smaller villages
of Tarasp and Vulpera. Sandwiched between the valley
road and the north bank of the En River, Scuol is divided
into two distinct halves but the lower part is the core of
the old village. There are some charming examples of
Engadine houses dating from the 17th century, built
around two paved squares. In the most imposing of these
buildings, the **Chagronda**, opposite the 16th-century
church, is housed a museum devoted to the history of the
Lower Engadine. The two bridges crossing to Vulpera are
interesting – the lower one being of the roofed wooden
type not characteristic of the region.

In winter the sunny, south-facing slopes of Motta
Naluns provide a number of gentle runs for predominantly
Swiss and German skiers.

THUSIS

A busy market town at the foot
of the Heinzenberg, Thusis is a
major junction in the Domleschg
Valley. Formerly a health resort
of some repute, it now
attracts more climbers than
convalescents, drawn largely by
the rocky pyramid of Piz Beverin
to the southwest. The town's
late-Gothic church dates from
1506 and the only other building
of significance is the ruined
11th-century castle of Hohen-
Rhaetian on a rocky outcrop
south of the town. On the
northern face of the same rock
are the ruins of the church of St
John, destroyed in the 15th
century. Thusis is surrounded by
thickly wooded hills and tiny
pastoral communities set among
lovely orchards high upon the
eastern wall of the Domleschg
Valley. Many of these are close
to more ruins of ancient feudal
fortresses, the most notable
being at Rothenbrunnen,
Paspels and Rodels.

ZUOZ

The influence of the Planta family in this old Engadine
village is clearly visible. The cobbled streets are very
narrow, admitting little sunlight and lined by ancient,
16th-century buildings, shuttered and painted in the
distinctive Engadine style. The fountain in the main square
is surmounted by a bear, the heraldic symbol of the
Plantas, and one that is repeated throughout much of the
valley. The village's Romanesque church, rebuilt in the
early 16th century, provides a distinctive landmark with its
tall, finely tapered spire. On the northern perimeter of the
square is the most imposing building in the village, the
former Planta residence with its 13th-century tower
connected by arcades.

Formerly the capital of the Upper Engadine, Zuoz is
now a summer resort of some importance. It is also
traditionally a centre of education, now the home of
the legendary Lyceum Alpinum, Switzerland's finest
private school.

Via Maistra
☎ 081 854 1510

*The graceful tower of
Zuoz's Romanesque
church is the town's
landmark*

Railways &
Scenic Journeys

Railways and mountains do not mix. It was clear from the start that this was true. Metal wheel on metal rail did not generate the friction required to climb hills and so gradients were eliminated by meticulous surveying that ensured that the track remained level. It was clear to everyone that the railway could reach the base of mountains but there it should stop. Clear to everyone that is except the Swiss. In a country that mixes flat land with some of the highest mountains in Europe the perceived wisdom could not apply. The Swiss needed to link the various parts of their country and so if there was mountain in the way they would tunnel through it, if a chasm needed to be crossed they would bridge it, and if the slope was too steep for a conventional train, then a different sort of train was needed. The result was the creation of railways that explore some of the most ruggedly beautiful scenery in Europe.

Though perhaps not the most breathtakingly spectacular (though some will argue this point), the most unlikely railway is the **Bernese Oberland line**, which links Interlaken to the Lauterbrunnen and Grindelwald valleys, and then to the Jungfraujoch by tunnelling through Europe's most infamous mountain, the Eiger. The impetus for the creation of this railway was tourism rather than a desire to ease the lot of the farmers of the alpine meadows below the great peaks, and there were some who opposed the line on the grounds that tourists would ruin for the ever the pastoral haven of the valleys. But commerce prevailed and lines were opened to Lauterbrunnen and Grindelwald in 1890, the link to Kleine Scheidegg being made three years later. In that same year,

There are plenty of photo opportunites when you take a scenic rail journey through Switzerland

1893, Adolf Guyer-Zeller looked across to the great peaks from the Schilthorn and perceived the audacious place to tunnel through the Eiger. Work began in 1896 and was completed in 1912.

At Interlaken visitors change from the Swiss main line to the metre gauge mountain railway. First stop is Wilderswil from where the Riggenbach rack-railway climbs to Schynige Platte and a spectacular view of the Oberland peaks. The pretty village of Lauterbrunnen stands at the entrance to a valley famous for its waterfalls, the Trümmelbach falling in a series of cascades, while the Staubbach takes one spectacular leap of 300m. The restaurant at the top of the Schilthorn (reached by cable car) was the setting for part of the James Bond film *On Her Majesty's Service*.

From Lauterbrunnen the train climbs through woodland, with occasional stunning views of the valley and the Staubbach, to reach Wengen. The usefulness of the line to visitors is easy to appreciate at the stops of Allmend and Wengernalp where walkers leave and join. It was at Wengernalp's hotel that Byron wrote **Manfred**, published in 1817, which brought the first wave of tourists to the Bernese Oberland and so played a part in the creation of the railway. Beyond Wengen the view opens up as the line rises towards the great peaks. Kleine Scheidegg is little more than a railway station, a hotel and a small collection of shops, but is one of the most spectacular settings of any Swiss hamlet. Looking towards Grindelwald, to the left is the Lauberhorn, famous as the setting for one of the downhill skiing season's most famous classics while to the right is the north wall of the Eiger. The telescope at Kleine Scheidegg offered a grandstand views of the epics and tragedies played out on the wall, adding to its notoriety.

At Kleine Scheidegg visitors change trains for the ride to the Jungfraujoch. There is a brief stop at Eigergletscher (where the glacier of the name has retreated recently, in common with most Oberland glaciers) before the Eiger tunnel is entered. The tunnel took 14 years to bore and is 7.1km long with gradients of up to 25 per cent. There are two stops in the tunnel. The first window allows a view of the Eiger north face. Though not on part of the famous climb it does allow an appreciation of the steepness and make-up of the wall. At the second stop, Eismeer, the view is the cold, ice-shrouded world of the high peaks.

Jungfraujoch is Europe's highest railway station at 3,454m (11,333ft) high enough for altitude to be a problem – walk slowly to avoid breathlessness and, possibly, a headache. The views from the top of the Sphinx Observatory of the Aletsch Glacier, Europe's longest, and the Bernese Oberland peaks, are among the finest in Switzerland.

From Kleine Scheidegg the line descends to Grindelwald. To the left in winter skiers usually overtake

NAMES

The trio of famous Bernese Oberland peaks is named for a Swiss folk tale in which a young girl (Jungfrau) is saved from the clutches of an ogre (Eiger) by a wily old monk (Monch). By contrast the town of Interlaken is named for the most mundane of reasons, its position 'between lakes', the lakes of Thun and Brienz.

the chugging trains. To the right the view of the Eiger's north face is often shut out by canopies that shield the line from drifting snow, but such glimpses as are possible suggest the face is awesomely big. At Grund the train reverses (or visitors may change trains) for the short ascent to Grindelwald. From here the circuit is completed along the less spectacular, but still delightful, line to Wilderswil and Interlaken.

If the Jungfrau railways are Switzerland's most unlikely, its most famous is the **Glacier Express**, which links the resorts of St Moritz and Zermatt through the rugged scenery of Grisons and the Valais. Historically the route started with the construction of the line from Visp to Zermatt in 1899 and was completed in 1915 with a new section near the Furka Pass. Early journeys were a prey to bad weather, many of the bridges being dismantled during the winter to stop their demolition by avalanches, the route only being opened when spring allowed rebuilding. Vast avalanche deflectors were needed to ensure that winter services could be maintained and only in 1982 with the construction of the 13km Furka Base Tunnel – Europe's longest single track tunnel – was the route finally 'completed'. With over 90 viaducts, almost 300 bridges, and the tunnels the Glacier Express is a wonder of engineering as well as trip through a wonderland of nature.

Yet the Glacier Express is not a complete journey in the way of the Jungfrau line, since parts of the journey are along sections of the Swiss railway network. Some carriages make the journey all the way, but some visitors will find they need to change at Chur and Visp.

St Moritz, beneath the glitz, is a pleasant, traditional Swiss resort set at the edge of a lake and with a backdrop of the Engadine peaks. The journey starts in Engadine, following a level line to Samedan, before entering the first tunnel, the 5.9km Albulatunnel beyond which, to avoid using a rack, the engineers constructed a series of loops and spiral tunnels to link the tunnel entrance with Bergün. This is one of the journey's most dramatic sections, though the constant rocking as the train switches direction is not to every traveller's taste. The descent continues to the Landwasser viaduct, gracefully curved but apparently defying gravity as it crosses high above the river. Next is another dramatic section of line where it crosses the Schyn Ravine through tunnels and over viaducts. This section of track stumped the builders for almost a decade until, with the alternatives proving even worse, they tackled the ravine head-on.

The line now descends through gentler country, travellers relaxing and needing fewer superlatives for

HEIDE EXPRESS & ENGADINE STAR

The section of the Glacier Express from St Moritz to Reichenau is also part of a circular journey known as the Heide Express and of the Engadine Star. Each uses part of the Swiss main line to reach Chur and Landquart from where the two routes head east through a broad valley to Malons. Beyond that village and the next, the line follows the Landquart River through a narrow, spectacular gorge, then heads up through wooded country to reach Klosters. From Klosters the Engadine Star heads east, taking the recently opened Vereina Tunnel to reach Susch, Zernez and the Swiss National Park, an area of mountain and cembran pine in which red deer, roe deer and ibex wander. From Klosters the Heide Express heads south to Davos and then on to Filisur and the Glacier Express route.

the view as the junction of Reichenau is reached. Look high and left for a glimpse of the 12th century Hohenrätien castle which featured in several of Turner's paintings. In spring the journey from Reichenau to Ilanz and Treen is through orchards rich in blossom, with the infant Rhine as companion. Soon farmland gives way to barren mountains as the train climbs towards Oberalp Pass, the view sometimes obscured by the avalanche canopies. Beyond the pass (at 2048m), the descent is even steeper, with rack-and pinion occasionally needed to help the train reach Andermatt, a pretty town at the junction of alpine pass roads and railways.

From Realp, west of Andermatt, the line rose to the old Furka Pass tunnel, but this section was difficult to keep open in winter, as was the road over the pass. The solution was the drilling of the new Furka Base Tunnel which takes cars through the mountain in winter. From the far side there are stunning views of the Rhône Glacier, birthplace of both the river and the name of the Express. The line now follows the river through the high Valais. At Fiesch the earliest known version of the legend of William Tell is depicted in a late 16th century fresco on the Tellenhaus. Beyond is Brig, a railway junction from where the Simplon line heads south along a route pioneered by Napoleon to reach Italy and Lake Maggiore. Our journey continues to Visp where the Rhône Valley is ignored in favour of a sharp left turn into the Mattertal. For all that the scenery close to St Moritz and Andermatt is marvellous, for many the finest part of the journey now lies ahead. The line is at its steepest here and the valley is so tight beyond Stalden's bridge that the walls on either side can be touched by leaning out of the window – or so it seems. At Tasch the valley road ends, motorists joining the train for the climb to Zermatt. Marmots can be seen (or their whistling heard) in the meadows beside the line and then, as a corner is rounded, the Matterhorn comes into view. Not Europe's highest mountain, but certainly its most

> ### RACE TO THE TOP
>
> The race to be the first to climb the Matterhorn occupied several years with English climbers John Tyndall and Edward Whymper and Italian guide Jean Carrel attempting the peak many times before Whymper was successful in 1865. Whymper's success turned into tragedy with four of his team of seven being killed on the descent, the deaths leading to recriminations among the survivors and an attempt by Queen Victoria to have mountaineering banned.

Taking the St Moritz Mountain Railway up to Corviglia

striking, the Matterhorn rears up above Zermatt, an achingly beautiful village. Zermatt is the terminus of the Glacier Express, but it is not the end of our journey as the Gornergrat rack-and-pinion line, opened in 1898, continues upwards. It rises 1480m in its 9.4km, using 5 viaducts, 5 bridges and 5 tunnels to reach Gornergrat at 3092m and an even more spectacular view of the Matterhorn.

The **William Tell Express** links Lucerne to Italian-speaking Switzerland. Lucerne, the capital of Napoleon's Helvetian Republic, is at the centre of the region where the 'Perpetual Alliance', the foundation of modern Switzerland, was agreed. As Wilhelm Tell, an almost certainly mythical character, but one who embodies Swiss nationalism, came from this area it is natural to take his name on a journey which explores the Swiss heartland. The Express starts, strangely for a rail journey, with a ride on a paddle steamer from Lucerne along the length of Lake Lucerne to Flüellen. There the train is boarded for the journey south to Andermatt. Beyond the town the train climbs through increasingly barren, but bold scenery to reach the Gotthard Tunnel and, beyond, Airolo once a pack-horse station and now the highest station of the Swiss Federal Railway network at 1142m.

The road-marred valley is now followed downhill. At Biasca the valley has broadened enough to lose the road view and take in some lovely waterfalls. Crossing the canton border into Ticino, Bellinzona, Ticino's capital, is soon reached. From here branches of the line go south to Lugano, an elegant, sophisticated city at the edge of a mountain-surrounded lake that bears the same name, or west to Locarno at the tip of Lake Maggiore which Switzerland shares with Italy.

Those wanting to continue by rail through spectacular scenery of interconnecting gorges and valleys, can now take the **Centovalli Express**, which leaves Locarno and travels through Italy to reach Domodossola at the foot of the Simplon Pass. For a round trip, from Domodossola the journey can be continued through the Simplon Tunnel to Brig for a connection to Andermatt.

Though these journeys are the most famous, they are not a complete list of what Switzerland has to offer. From Montreux the **Swiss Chocolate Train** climbs to Gruyères (home of the famous cheese) and on to Broc and the Nestlé chocolate factory, while in the north of the country the **Voralpen Express** links Romanshorn on Lake Constance with Lucerne. Each is as delightful and worthwhile as the more famous journeys. Though its geography seems to argue against rail travel, any of journeys enhances an exploration of one of Europe's most scenically stunning countries.

GOLDEN PASS

Lucerne is also the start point for the Golden Pass line. The journey begins through typical mid-Switzerland farmland as far as Sarnen. At Alpnachstad the journey can be broken to enjoy the delights of the world's steepest rack railway that follows the 4.3m and occasionally 48 per cent track to Pilatus. Beyond Sarnen the Golden Pass skirts the shore of Sarnen See to Giswil before entering distinctly more rugged country, climbing to Brünig and then descending to Meiringen. Next come Interlaken and the shores of Lake Thun to Spiez. Mountain scenery now returns as the train climbs to Saanenmöser and the high point on the line. The descent to Gstaad involves crossing a three-span truss viaduct, one of the landmarks of the route. Beyond Gstaad the equally famous Châteaux d'Oex is reached before the line climbs again, tunnelling under the Col de Jaman to descend to Montreux.

Glaciers

Of the great natural phenomena that characterise the Swiss landscape, its glaciers must rank among the most impressive. Their attendant neighbours – mountains – have a quite different effect on the beholder: they may impress, they may inspire, they may often instil fear, but they do not move.

Glaciers are slowly rolling rivers of ice that advance or retreat in response to varying climatic conditions. The sensation of standing on or beneath one, aware of its imperceptible movement, is at once unnerving and strangely bewitching. Glaciers are essentially destructive forces that move forward under their own weight, pulverising everything in their path. Fortunately, their progress in the Alps is slow – generally no more than a few centimetres a day – and their pattern of movement is usually predictable. In some parts of the world, however, glaciers can move very rapidly – as much as 8kph.

The two largest glaciers in the Alps are both in the Valais – the **Aletsch**, rolling down from beneath the Jungfrau to the upper flanks of the Goms Valley for 23.5km, and the 14.5km-long **Gorner** at Zermatt. However, by Antarctica standards these are small.

A glacier is formed when snow accumulates above the 'snow line', defined as the lower limit of perpetual snow; in the Swiss Alps it lies between 2,500 and 3,200m. Continually fed by fresh snowfalls, the snow is gradually compacted into ice by pressure. The layers of this new snow on the surface of the glacier build up until the weight of the accumulation exceeds the strength of the ice. At this point the ice-mass at the base of the glacier begins to move slowly, its speed dependent on the gradient of the slope and the temperature of the ice. The

GLACIAL FACTS

Any large mass of permanent, shifting ice that forms on land through the re-crystallisation of snow may be characterised as a glacier. Occupying about 11 per cent of the earth's total land surface, but comprising about 75 per cent of its fresh water, the vast majority of this perennial ice is concentrated in Antarctica and Greenland.

The remainder is widely spread throughout the world's continents (with the exception of Australia). It is estimated that as many as 200,000 glaciers exist in various parts of the world; about 600 of them are in the Swiss Alps, covering an area of approximately 2,000sq km.

Above: *detail of the structure of the Rhone glacier in the Furka Pass near the Italian border*

Left: *the Stein glacier and Susten Pass in the Obwalden canton*

Looking down into the steep upper reaches of the Grindelwald Glacier in the Jungfrau region

THE DANGERS

Many thousands of climbers and skiers have discovered to their cost that should they survive a fall of anything up to 60m into the heart of a glacier any hope of rescue is generally a forlorn one. Bodies of victims are sometimes found many years later, in remarkable states of preservation, as the glacier disgorges them at its side or terminus. In some instances, 19th-century climbers (where identification is possible from their possessions) have been interred over a century after their death by their own distant descendants. The 5,000-year-old 'Iceman', found by hikers on the perimeter of a glacier on the Austrian-Italian border, is the most dramatic example of how this macabre process of freezing entombment works.

movement of the Alps' valley glaciers is similar to that of the flow of a river, with velocity greater in the centre than at the sides. The upper layers of hard, brittle ice are carried by the mobile icepack below, which, as it moves, causes the surface to fracture into wide fissures known as crevasses. Often concealed by flimsy 'snow bridges', these open and close according to the pulling action of the ice. They represent unquestionably the most dangerous area of the glacier. The irony of the treacherous nature of crevasses is that they also provide the most pleasing of spectacles for observers (from a safe distance). Frequently, they take the form of jagged pinnacles and towers as the upper surface of the glacier is broken up into a chaos of ice sculptures.

At the melting tip or snout, of the glacier, amid piles of rocky detritus, water is discharged in a distinctive milky-coloured flow, a feature caused by the fine stone-dust created by the abrasive grinding action of the glacier and its contents. Often the flow takes the form of a spectacular and turbulent torrent, in other cases it is little more than a turbid trickle. But the real glory of a glacier lies not so much at its end as in the extraordinary depth and range of colours in the ice formations of its body. Inexpressibly beautiful shades of blue and green combine to create one of the most spectacular features of the Swiss landscape.

Winter Sports

It was largely due to the patronage of the British – and the ingenuity of the Swiss – that winter sport developed from an essentially parochial pastime into a multi-billion-pound global industry. If the Scandinavian countries were the nurseries of winter sports, then the finishing school – like all good finishing schools – was in Switzerland.

Skating is the oldest of the winter sports to be developed in the Swiss Alps. Originating with the Dutch, who realised the advantages of travelling on frozen canals with crude skates made of bone, wood and metal. By the 17th century skating was becoming an established sport not only throughout northern Europe but also in the United States and Canada. In Switzerland at this time the main skating centres were St Moritz, Davos and Grindelwald. Today there are skating rinks in nearly every Alpine resort, and some of the finest natural rinks in the world are high up in the Swiss Alps on frozen lakes.

But it was the sport of **tobogganing**, believed to have originated in the American Indian territories, that came to satisfy the early winter-sports pioneers' craving for speed and danger. Imported to the Swiss Alps by the British, the first recorded organised races took place in Davos in February 1883. Quickly recognising that the practice of starting all competitors together was unacceptably dangerous, the British made the far-sighted decision to minimise the risk of collision with fellow competitors by constructing a purpose-built 1.2km run in St Moritz and timing each tobogganer's descent. This development laid the groundwork for the 'staggered' competition in downhill winter sports over the next century. To this day the toboggan course known as the Cresta Run follows more or less its original route, and it is still operated by the British.

Another major winter sport to be introduced to the Swiss Alps at this time was **curling**, variously claimed to be the invention of the Dutch, the Germans and the Scots. Records prove that the latter were sliding the heavy stones across ice from as early as the beginning of the 16th century. In 1880 the first Swiss curling club was founded in St Moritz, and today there are more than 150 curling rinks throughout the country.

The most significant, addition to the winter sports scene in the Swiss Alps was **skiing**. It was not until the late 1800s that the real skiing revolution began to take root

---

SNOW TRAVEL

Probably even before the invention of the wheel various devices were already being used to aid men's progress across snow and ice. Rock drawings found in Norway indicate that skates, skis and rudimentary sledges have been in use for over 4,500 years. However, with the exception of skating, these were practical solutions for overcoming physical difficulties. It was not until the late 19th century that the sporting potential of travelling at speed over ice and snow was fully realised.

Sledge runs on the Schatzalp and Rinerhorn

SKI INNOVATION

Who invented skis, and when, will probably remain undiscovered, but the earliest hard evidence suggests that they originated in Scandinavia. In a 'gentleman's' ski competition in Oslo, a semi-literate peasant called Sondre Norheim turned up and won every race. The secret of his apparently effortless success was a ski he had designed himself. It had a waist, was considerably shorter than the traditional ski in use at that time, and it had a binding that held the foot securely to the ski. As a result the ski became fully manoeuvrable for the first time using the turning technique that came to be known as the 'Telemark', after the mountain on which it was developed.

at the first-generation ski resorts of St Moritz, Flims, Arosa, Zermatt and Grindelwald. It was still very much a sport of limited appeal, with hours of plodding uphill rewarded by a brief, albeit exhilarating, descent of only a few minutes. In the early 1900s another of the turning points in the burgeoning industry occurred with the arrival of the British travel operator, Henry Lunn. The inventor of the modern 'package' holiday, Lunn began to bring over groups under the auspices of the unashamedly elitist name of the Public Schools Alpine Sports Club. By the 1920s, the resorts of Wengen, Mürren and Grindelwald had been so thoroughly colonised by the British upper classes that the bemused Swiss claimed that they needed a passport to enter. Various ski clubs sprang up at this time, coinciding with the novel concept of 'downhill only' skiing inaugurated by the British. Persuading the Jungfrau railway authorities to connect Wengen and Grindelwald via the col of Kleine Scheidegg, the new generation of skiers were able to ski downhill into either village without any of the strenuous climbing that had previously been necessary. An even more radical development was the first draglift, designed and installed in Davos in 1934. This T-bar took 30 seconds to convey skiers up slopes that had previously necessitated a 20-minute climb.

Today, millions make an annual pilgrimage to the Swiss Alps – still unrivalled for the variety of winter sports, the beauty of their setting, and the traditional charm of the world's first ski resorts.

Snow-boarding in deep-snow conditions

Where To...

Above: *Swiss flag flying over Lake Thun*
Right: *Sign for 'Abbaye de l'Aigle Noir' at Aigle*

Hotels

Prices
Prices indicated below are for a double room including breakfast (in high season, which will include both summer and winter for some towns).

£££ = more than CHF270
££ = CHF203-CHF270
£ = under CHF203

Classification
The Swiss hotel classification system uses 1 to 5 stars, the definitions being

* simple
** comfortable
*** good middle class
**** first class
***** luxury

The system seems straightforward, but is not. For a list of facilities ranging from night service to frequency of changing of bed linen certain standards are required for any star rating and all of these must be achieved for the star rating to be granted. So it is worth looking at the list to see how your needs measure up to the requirements.

Northern Switzerland

Basel
Drei Könige (£££)
Magnificently sited beside the river. You may feel like the king of the name after joining Picasso and Mick Jagger in the roll of those who have stayed. The downside is the hole in the wallet. There are two restaurants that are as good as would be expected.
✉ **Blumenrain 8** ☎ **061 260 5050; fax 061 260 5060**

Zürich
Adler (££)
The most expensive hotels in this most expensive of cities tend to be away from the centre, which can often be noisy at night. This charming hotel, with frescoed walls, is close to the lake and to the quays (for many the most picturesque part of the city). Good soundproofing ensures a comfortable night. Excellent restaurant serving typical Swiss food.
✉ **Rosengasse 10, am Hirschplatz** ☎ **01 2669 696; fax 01 266 9669**

Bernese Oberland

Bern
Allegro (£££)
Not cheap, but some rooms have great views of the old town and others equally good ones of the Oberland peaks. Three restaurants with a choice varying from Asian to Swiss.
✉ **Kornhaustrasse 3** ☎ **031 339 5500; fax 031 339 5510**

Martahaus (£)
A comfortable hotel about 10 minutes walk from the centre of the city. Tall and old, but refurbished in good, if somewhat dull, style. Well run.
✉ **Wyttenbachstrasse 22A** ☎ **031 332 4135; fax 031 333 3386**

Grindelwald
Wolter (££)
One of the best locations in town, close to the station, and in winter the skibus stops outside. Family run and very comfortable. The restaurant is excellent, serving good, unfussy food.
✉ **3818 Grindelwald** ☎ **033 854 3333; fax 033 854 3339**

Interlaken
Beau-Site (££)
Conveniently close to West railway station, this hotel has tremendous views of the Jungfrau and nearby peaks. The gardens have seats and parasols for the summer. Very clean and comfortable rooms (some with mountain views).
✉ **Seestrasse 16** ☎ **033 826 7575; fax 033 826 7585**

Kandersteg
Adler (££)
Delightful Swiss-chalet style establishment with an open fire in the lounge. Most rooms have private balconies to make the most of the position. Two good restaurants. Winter visitors will love the bar for après-ski.
✉ **Hauptstrasse** ☎ **033 675 8010; fax 033 675 8011**

Wengen
Eden (£)
Short walk from the centre in a very quiet area (as most hotels in traffic-free Wengen

are). Very pleasant rooms, though not all have private showers. Some private balconies.

 3823 Wengen ☎ 033 855 1634; fax 033 855 3950

Central Switzerland

Altdorf
Bahnhof (£)
Family-run hotel in an old house with a new extension. Short walk from the famous William Tell statue. There are limited facilities, but the rooms are pleasant and the staff very nice. Good restaurant

✉ 6460 Altdorf ☎ 041 870 1032; fax 041 870 9932

Luzern
Schweizerhof (£££)
Without doubt the best location in town, overlooking the lake and within a short distance of the Kapellbrücke. This quality hotel offers everything you would expect in terms of comfort and facilities.

✉ Schweizerhofquai 3 ☎ 041 410 0410; fax 041 410 2971

Rebstock (££)
Close to the Hofkirche, the lake and Schweizerhofquai, this extremely attractive building dates from the 12th century and has excellent decor, rooms and service. There are two good restaurants – the Swiss one is especially worth a try.

✉ Sankt Leodegar Platz 3 ☎ 041 410 3581; fax 041 410 3917

Alpha (£)
Not the best looking place in town, but very pleasant

inside. Conveniently located about a 10 minute walk from the centre and close to the railway station.

✉ Zähringstrasse 24 ☎ 041 240 4280; fax 041 240 9131

Schwyz
Wysses Rössli (££)
In a delightful position across from St Martin's Church. Very well appointed, good service and two excellent restaurants.

✉ Hauptplatz 3 ☎ 041 811 1922; fax 041 811 1046

Lac Genève

Genève
Edelweiss (££)
Close to Quai President Wilson and within walking distance of all the main sites. Tall and elegant, with a contrasting rather rustic interior (it qualifies as a 'ambiance chalet'), which is very comfortable and pleasant.

✉ Place de la Navigation 2 ☎ 022 544 5151; fax 022 544 5199

Lausanne
Hotel de la Paix (£££)
Beautifully positioned and beautifully elegant. You will find everything you would expect of a luxury hotel including a superb restaurant. Try to get a room facing the lake.

✉ Avenue Benjamin-Constant 5 ☎ 021 310 7171; fax 021 310 7172

Montreux
Hostellerie du Lac (££)
As the name suggests, right on the lake front just a minute or two from the casino. The owner goes out of his way to keep it friendly

Camping
Camping is only available on authorised sites. If you are interested in camping in Switzerland a map and list is available from the Swiss National Tourist Office. Those interested in caravaning in Switzerland will need a similar list, available from the Schweizer Camping und Caravaning Verband,

✉ Habsburgerstrasse 35, CH-6004 Luzern
☎ 041 234 822.

Velotels
As the name implies, these are hotels specifically for cyclists. They can be recognised by their sign, but a lst is available by telephoning
☎ 01 680 2223; fax 01 780 6564

Young Persons Accommodation

Switzerland has a limited number of excellent Youth Hostels, details of which are available from a visitor's home country association. In addition there is the Swiss Family Experiment, which involves interested Swiss families offering rooms to young people on a one to three week basis. Details are available from the Swiss National Tourist Office. This system is quite different from the zimmer sign that is seen on private houses throughout Switzerland. These signs indicate accommodation on a bed and breakfast basis that is available to all travellers.

and cosy and succeeds admirably. There are several good restaurants within walking distance.

✉ **Rue du Quai 12** ☎ **021 963 3271; fax 021 963 1835**

Ticino

Locarno

Beau-Rivage (££)

Imposing building on the lake front road. The interior is very elegant and many of the rooms, which are furnished in the local style (natural wood), have lake views – though these tend to be smaller than the ones without. Excellent buffet breakfast.

✉ **Viale Verbano 31** ☎ **091 743 1355; fax 091 749 409**

Dell'Angelo (£)

Situated at the southern end of Piazza Grande, close to the castle. Housed in a completely renovated 17th-century building, the Dell'Angelo is surprisingly inexpensive for its location and amenities, though the furnishing is basic rather than grand.

✉ **Piazza Grande 1** ☎ **091 751 8175; fax 091 751 8256**

Lugano

Grand Hotel Villa Castagnola (£££)

As luxurious as the name implies, the marble-clad public rooms and tropical park merely enhance the overall feel of this sumptuous hotel. The rooms are superb, have lovely lake and park views, and the excellent restaurant complements them perfectly.

✉ **Viale Castagnola 31** ☎ **091 973 2555; fax 091 973 2550**

Hotel du Lac (££)

A somewhat banal name, but one that accurately describes the hotel's position in Paradiso, the southern suburb of Lugano. The hotel owns a section of the lakeside for private swimming. Very comfortable rooms, all with lake view.

✉ **Riva Paradiso 3** ☎ **091 994 1921; fax 091 994 1122**

Morcote

Carina Carlton (£££)

A special place for those with an interest in architecture as it was once owned by Gaspare Fossati, a famous Swiss architect whose leanings towards Ottoman style are obvious throughout. The hotel also has a terrific Italianate facade. The rooms are well furnished (some of the antiques are real) and many have great views over the lake. There is a lakeview terrace too.

✉ **Via Cantonale** ☎ **091 996 1131; fax 091 996 1929**

Valais & Vaud

Brig

Schlosshotel (£)

Ideal for those wishing to tour the Valais as it is easy to locate and has garage parking. Comfortable and close to many restaurants.

✉ **Kirchgasse 4** ☎ **027 922 9595; fax 027 922 9596**

Château d'Oex

Ermitage (££)

Very pleasant hotel that, as might be expected, is difficult to get into during the balloon festival in January without booking well in advance. The rooms are very comfortable and the restaurant is good.

Le Petit Pré ☎ 026 924
6003; fax 026 924 5076

Saas Fee
Allalin (££)
One of the more attractive
hotels in this delightful
village. Well-furnished and
comfortable rooms. The
restaurant is justly famous
for its Valais cuisine.

✉ **3906 Saas Fee** ☎ 027 957
1815; fax 027 957 3115

Verbier
Hotel de la Poste (££)
Located very close to the
main square. Family run and
particularly suitable for
families in a resort that
otherwise concentrates on
adult visitors. The rooms are
decorated in alpine style (but
the modern rather than the
old style). Very pleasant
restaurant.

✉ **Rue de Médran** ☎ 027
771 6681; fax 027 771 3401

Zermatt
Grand Hotel Zermatterhof (£££)
Come here for that once-in-a-
lifetime treat, starting with a
horse-drawn carriage to
collect you at the station.
Every possible facility is
offered and the rooms have
many luxuries. The
restaurant is one of the best
places in town to eat.

✉ **3920 Zermatt** ☎ 027 966
6600; fax 027 966 6699

Garni Tannenhof (££)
A good deal easier on the
average pocket, this simple
but very pleasant hotel is
well decorated and
maintained, and has a
friendly atmosphere.

✉ **Bahnhofstrasse** ☎ 027
967 3188; fax 027 967 2173

Grisons

Davos
Ochsen (££)
Close to the railway station
and so a little way from the
centre. Simple, but
extremely cosy and friendly.
Some rooms – all of which
are well furnished – look out
on to the Jakobshorn. Good,
inexpensive restaurant.

✉ **Talstrasse 10 7270 Davos-
Platz** ☎ 081 413 5222; fax 081
413 7671

Klosters
Rustico (££)
Sometimes described as a
restaurant with rooms, but
that is unfair as the rooms
are comfortable and the
overall level of service
excellent. The restaurant is
definitely one of the less
showy, but very good
eateries in town.

✉ **Landstrasse 194** ☎ 081
422 1212; fax 081 422 5355

St Moritz
Crystal (£££)
The hotel looks a little out of
place among the period
buildings near the Corviglia
cog railway, but don't be put
off, the Crystal is a lovely
place with authentic alpine
furnishings in both the public
places and the rooms. Very
good Italian restaurant.

✉ **Via Traunter Plazzas 1**
☎ 081 836 2626; fax 081
836 2627

Waldhaus am See (££)
Once an inn, then a private
house, now a fine hotel. The
rooms are very comfortable
and those eating in will enjoy
the beautiful decor in the
restaurant.

✉ **Via Dimlej 6** ☎ 081 836
6000; fax: 081 836 6060

Mountain Huts
With so many mountains
of such quality it is no
surprise that the Swiss
have an Alpine Club and,
as with the other
mountainous countries of
Europe, the club owns
and runs huts in the
mountains. The Swiss
National Tourist Office
has a list, but better
information is available
from Schweizer Alpenclub
✉ Monbijoustrasse 61,
CH-3000 Bern 23
☎ 031 370 1818

Disabled Visitors
The Swiss National
Tourist Office publishes a
fact sheet for disabled
travellers and a list of
hotels where rooms
specifically suited to the
disabled are available.
Inevitably the pressure on
these rooms is
considerable and it is
advisable to book well in
advance of your journey.

Restaurants

Prices
Approximate prices per person for a three course meal excluding wine:

£££ = more than CHF82
££ = CHF54-CHF82
£ = under CHF54

Quality
Irrespective of the standard of the restaurant, Swiss eateries are almost without exception clean and well run. The kitchens will be spotless and the service efficient. It is a well-known joke at the expense of the Swiss that they are efficient to the point of mania. In food preparation and in serving that reputation proves to be advantages.

Northern Switzerland

Basel

Zum Goldenen Sternen (££)
The oldest restaurant in town dating from the 15th century. Close to the Rhine and the Gegenwartskunst (Contemporary Art Museum). Traditional Swiss menu but with distinct French leanings. The smoked eel and trout are specialities. Booking recommended.
✉ At Alban-Rheinweg 70
☎ 061 272 1666 🕐 Closed for 10 days before Christmas

Da Roberto (£)
Very good Italian restaurant popular with non-smokers and the young. Pizzas and pasta specialities, nothing too fancy, but excellent value for money
✉ Kuchengasse 3
☎ 061 205 8550

Zürich

Kronenhalle (££)
The most famous restaurant in the city, but not the most expensive. The art, by such famous names as Braque, Klee, Miró and Picasso is original and gives an idea of the past clientele who have enjoyed the Swiss/French cuisine served here. Specialities include boiled beef and smoked pork. It is advisable to book.
✉ Rämistrasse 4, 8001
☎ 01 2516 6691

Bernese Oberland

Bern

Wein und Sein (££)
Currently the place to be seen in Bern. Not cheap but very good. The kitchen is in full view, which is always a good sign. A limited menu is posted on the wall but changes daily.
✉ Münstergasse 50 ☎ 031 311 9844 🕐 Closed Sun, Mon & 2 weeks late Jul

Arlequin (££)
The other place to be seen, though it has always been popular with the discerning. Swiss/Italian cooking in traditional decor. Very pleasant and worthwhile. Booking recommended.
✉ Gerechtigkeitsgasse 51
☎ 031 311 3946

Kornhauskeller (£)
Vast converted grain warehouse serving very good local cuisine. But you may need to wave your arms to attract the staff so big is the floor space. Live traditional music some evenings. Booking recommended.
✉ Kornhausplatz 18 ☎ 031 277 272 🕐 Closed Mon

Grindelwald

Alte Post (££)
One of the few Grindelwald restaurants that is not in a hotel. Lovely decor and very popular. Local cuisine with air-dried ham and anything with morels a particular favourite. Booking essential.
✉ 3818 Grindelwald
☎ 033 853 4242

Interlaken

Teene (££)
Unlikely as it might seem, this is a Swiss seafood restaurant, and a very good one. Lobster is a speciality, but the fish is good too. Book ahead.
✉ Alpenstrasse 58
☎ 033 822 9422

Schuh (££)

Very atmospheric – panoramic windows and a piano playing softly in the background. Swiss/Austrian cooking.

✉ Höheweg 56 ☎ 033 829 9441 🕓 Closed Nov & Mon Dec–Mar

Mürren
Piz Gloria (£)

At Piz Gloria customers can relive the James Bond film *On Her Majesty's Secret Service* while enjoying a straightforward, but excellent menu. Booking not required but only open if the cable car is operating.

✉ Schilthorn ☎ 033 856 2140

Wengen
Arvenstube (££)

Classic decor and Swiss menu. The specialities are fondue bourguignonne (pre-ordering essential) and Valais beef cooked at your table. Otherwise try the smoked breast of goose.

✉ Hotel Eiger ☎ 033 856 0505

Central Switzerland

Altdorf
Lehnhof (££)

Charming little place for both lunch and dinner. Bistro style, with a surprisingly extensive menu and excellent cooking.

✉ Lehnplatz 18 ☎ 041 870 1229 🕓 Closed first 2 weeks Jan & last week of Jul

Engelberg
Engelberg Hotel (££)

Excellent *stübli* in one of the nicer of the town's hotels. Very comfortable surroundings and a good menu.

✉ Dorfstrasse 14 ☎ 041 639 7969 🕓 Closed Wed

Luzern
Old Swiss House (£££)

One of the best places in the city. A beautiful old half-timbered building filled with antiques that add an air of splendour. People travel a long way to try the *Weinerschnitzel*, and no wonder. The rest of the menu is equally good.

✉ Löwenplatz 4 ☎ 041 410 6171

Stadtkeller (££)

Vast cellar with a history going back several hundred years. Live Swiss folk music usually enlivens the meal. The dishes are somewhat German with sauerkraut and sausage featuring prominently. The servings are also German style - very generous.

✉ Sternplatz 3 ☎ 041 410 4733 🕓 Closed Sun, Mon, all Nov & Mar

Schlössli Utenberg (££)

Terrific 18th-century baroque mansion about 4km northeast of the city on the road to Dietschiberg. Very atmospheric with a terrace overlooking Luzern. Good lunch menu.

✉ Utenbergstrasse 643 ☎ 041 420 0022 🕓 Closed Mon & Tue

Schwyz
Adelboden (££)

About 6km north of Schwyz on the road to Einsiedeln. Recommended for its typical Swiss alpine menu with both fish and meat dishes.

✉ Schlagstrasse, 6422 Steinen ☎ 041 832 1942 🕓 Closed Sun, Mon, 2 weeks Feb & late Jul/early Aug

Lac Genève

Genève
La Perle du Lac (£££)

Beautifully sited beside the lake in the excellent Mon Repos Park. Seating in the garden or in the quiet interior. Unusual dishes include fera (a lake fish) and

Tourist Menu

As well as the the a la carté menu virtually all restaurants offer a daily tourist menu, which is inexpensive and usually very good value. The choice will be limited, but if you are looking for something quick and affordable, particularly at lunchtime, then it is worth considering.

Specialities

With a country boasting distinctly French, German, Italian and Romansch areas it is no surprise that a journey across Switzerland can be a voyage through a range of cuisines. Veal (as schnitzel) and calf's liver are seen in most areas, but the national specialities are also available – *wurst* in the German areas, pastas in the Italian and mouthwatering sauces in the French.

119

Pain et Couvert

You will probably see *Pain et Couvert*, or, in the Italian part of the country, *Pane e Coperto*, added to your bill. This means 'bread and cover' and is the charge for use of the table and the bread basket that accompanies your meal. In theory the charge covers the basket no matter how many times you have it refilled. In practice, except in the most expensive restaurants you may not persuade the waiter to replace it once emptied (and you certainly won't a second time).

---

pigeon breast with duck liver and apricots. Booking essential.

✉ **Rue de Lausanne 126** ☎ **022 909 1020** 🕔 **Closed Mon & mid-Dec to mid-Jan**

Pizzeria da Paolo (£)

A complete contrast to La Perle; excellent pizzas and a good range of alternatives. Close to the water jet.

✉ **Rue de Lac 3** ☎ **022 736 3049**

Lausanne
La Jardin d'Asie (££)

Amazing place that offers Chinese, Malaysian and Japanese food. Also sushi and Asian cooking at its best. Highly recommended.

✉ **Avenue du Théâtre 7** ☎ **021 323 7484**

Montreux
L'Ermitage (£££)

In a suburb to the north-west, set in parkland close to the lake. Famous for its chef, Etienne Krebs, who offers such delights as lamb with alpine herbs and duck with a saute of local fungi.

✉ **Rue de Lac 75, Clarens** ☎ **021 964 4411**

Ticino

Ascona
Borromeo (££)

In a 14th-century monastery with a great outdoor terrace. The excellent Swiss and Italian cooking is popular with the locals. Try the Milanese risotto with saffron.

✉ **Via Collegio 16** ☎ **091 791 9281**

Locarno
Centenario (£££)

The best place in the city and one of the best restaurants in Switzerland. The simple dining room is perfectly in tune with the menu, which offers seasonal ingredients cooked in a straightforward fashion. The lamb with herbs

---

and deer with wild mushrooms are sensational, as is the fresh fruit souffle. Booking recommended.

✉ **Lungolago Motta 17** ☎ **091 743 8222** 🕔 **Closed Sun & Mon**

Boccalino (£)

Near to the castle and Piazza Grande is the best fish/vegetarian restaurant in the city. Very impressive menu and delightful surroundings.

✉ **Via della Motta 7** ☎ **091 751 9681** 🕔 **Closed dinner Sat–Mon, lunch Wed & Thu**

Lugano
Parco Saroli (££)

At the heart of the city. The inside is by a famous Swiss–Italian interior designer and gives the place a great ambiance. The food is good too.

✉ **Viale Stefano Franscini 6** ☎ **091 922 8805** 🕔 **Closed Sat & Sun**

Locanda bel Boschetto (££)

A rustic setting overflowing with flowers in season. Straightforward menu of fish and meat dishes cooked in full view over a 'barbecue'. Very pleasant atmosphere.

✉ **Via Boschetto 8, Cassarina** ☎ **091 994 4495**

Morcote
La Sorgente (£)

Extremely pleasant little restaurant at Vico about 4km northeast of Morcote, with outdoor dining in summer. Simple but excellent menu.

✉ **6921 Vico-Morcote** ☎ **091 996 2301**

Valais & Vaud

Brig
Schlosskeller (££)

Quaint place on the road to the Simplon Pass. Local cuisine in an unfussy way. Good for lunchtime eating.

✉ **Alte Simplonstrasse 26** ☎ **027 923 3352**

Fribourg
La Fleur-de-Lys (£££)
Excellent food served in equally impressive surroundings. The chef, Pierre-André Ayer, is famous for his ravioli and dishes incorporating lake perch.

✉ Rue des Forgerons 18
☎ 026 322 7961

Saas Fee
Swiss Chalet (££)
The name is appropriate for this fine restaurant at the northern end of town. Good food at reasonable prices.

✉ 3906 Saas Fee ☎ 027 957 3535

Verbier
Au Vieux Verbier (££)
Arguably the best restaurant in town that is not attached to a hotel. Close to the bottom of the ski slopes, which makes it crowded in winter. Excellent grilled fish and meat (steak flambéed at your table if you wish).

✉ Gare de Médran
☎ 027 771 1668

Zermatt
The Grill Room (£££)
In the Hotel Walliserhof. A former farmhouse that now houses a very fine restaurant serving Swiss, French and Italian cuisine, both meat and fish. Booking recommended.

✉ Hotel Walliserhof, Bahnhofstrasse ☎ 027 966 6555

Stockhorn (££)
Alpine decor, a blazing fire and a menu that includes raclette, pasta and meats.

✉ Riedstrasse ☎ 027 967 1747

Walliserkanne (£)
Delightful little place just a few steps from the railway station. The walls are an art gallery for local artists. The menu is Italian with pastas, pizzas and the more popular Italian meat dishes.

✉ Bahnhofstrasse
☎ 027 966 4610

Grisons

Arosa
Stueva-Cuolm (££)
A Tuscan trattoria in Switzerland. Very elegant and great food. It is claimed that the *daube de bouef* is marinated for 24 hours before serving.

✉ Poststrasse ☎ 081 378 8890

Davos
Bunderstübli (££)
Atmospheric restaurant with wood walls and a menu taken from old Swiss cookery books. The barley soup is outstanding.

✉ Dischmastrasse 8, 7260 Davos-Dorf ☎ 081 416 3393

Klosters
Alte Post (££)
The chance to see some of the celebrities that Klosters attracts adds a piquancy to the excellent menu of this attractive chalet restaurant. For something different, try the smoked trout with juniper. Book in advance.

✉ Doggilochstrasse 136
☎ 081 422 1716 🕐 Closed May & Nov

St Moritz
Jöhri's Talvo (£££)
A relative newcomer to the St Moritz scene, 3km southwest, which has established itself among top local restaurants. Local lamb in mountain herbs with mustard sauce is a favourite, but the *puschlav* ('poor man's soup') is exceptional.

✉ Via Gunels 15, 7512 Champfèr ☎ 081 833 4455

Engadina (£)
A sharp contrast (price-wise) to Jöhri's Talvo, but no less worthwhile. In the centre of Dorf, facing the town hall. Excellent fondues and some surprising things – snails in garlic butter for example.

✉ Piazza da Scuola 2

Wine
Wine is not a huge industry in Switzerland as it is in neighbouring countries, but some local varieties are worth sampling. Vaud is the best known wine-producing area, its whites being particularly good. Try Lavaux or Yvorne. Dôle is the most popular red wine in the country and, as with Fendant, a good white, it comes from the Valais. The Ticino wines are also worth trying, but be cautious as they are renowned for their very high alcohol content. Mezzana – both red and white – and the red Nostrano are excellent.

Shopping in Switzerland

Quality Time

Switzerland is world famous for its watches and clocks and these still represent one of the best buys for visitors. From the simple Swatch (early versions of which now change hands among collectors for hundreds of times their original price) to the most expensive makes, Switzerland is the place for choice – though not necessarily for price – being close to the source does not make them any cheaper.

Switzerland's superb products make it a shopper's paradise. Fine watches come in an infinte variety. More good buys are textiles, embroideries, fine handkerchiefs, woollen sportswear and linen. Chocolates tempt you with an amazing variety of sizes, shapes and flavours. Other interesting souvenirs include multi-blade pocket knives, music boxes, woodcarvings, ceramics and other handmade items, antiques and art books.

It is not possible to give a comprehensive list of shops in all the towns and villages in Switzerland, many of which have superb local craft and art works on offer. For the best of city shopping the following are worth a visit:

Basel

In Basel the best streets for shopping are Aeschenvorstadt, Freie Strasse, Gerbergasse, Schneidergasse and Spalenberg. There is an excellent market in Barfüsserplatz on Thursdays. For watches try Gübelin (⌧ Freie Strasse 27 ☎ 061 261 4033) if you have deep pockets or Kurz (⌧ Freie Strasse 39 ☎ 061 261 2620) if your taste is more modest. For leather Leder-Droeser (⌧ Eisengasse 11 ☎ 061 261 4253) is excellent for wallets, handbags etc. For shoes and clothing Bally Capitol zum Pflug (⌧ Freie Strasse 38 ☎ 061 261 1897) offers three floors of delights.

Bern

In Bern for the best shopping go to Spitalgasse, Postgasse, Marktgasse, Kramgasse and Gerechtigkeitgasse. Globus (⌧ 17 Spitalgasse ☎ 031 313 4040) is the main department store (and one of the best in the country). At Kramgasse 61 Oberlander Heimat (☎ 031 311 3000) is the best craft shop in town, with items from all over Switzerland, an excellent place for souvenirs and gifts. Ciolina Modehaus (⌧ Marktgasse 51 ☎ 031 328 6464) is excellent for ladies fashion. For leather head for Gypax Mode (⌧ Spitalgasse 4 ☎ 031 311 2561), while for quality jewellery try Gübelin (⌧ Bahnhofplatz 11 ☎ 031 311 5433).

Genève

When shopping in Genève head for Rue de Mont-Blanc, Rue Rousseau, Rue du Marché, Rue de Chatepoulet, Rue du Rhône and Rue de la Cité. These are where the designer shops are congregated. Chanel, Hermès, Bucherer and Bruno Magli are within touching distance of each other in Rue du Rhône. The best departmental stores are Bon Genie (⌧ Rue du Marché 34 ☎ 022 818 1111) and Globus (⌧ Rue du Rhône 48 ☎ 022 319 5050). For less exclusive ladies fashion, try Les Créateurs (⌧ Rue du Rhône 100 ☎ 022 311 5142). Gübelin, the upmarket jewellery company, has a shop at Rue du Rhône 60 (☎ 022 310 8655). Two great places for souvenirs and gifts are Come Prima (⌧ Rue de la Cité ☎ 022 310 7779) and the Swiss Tradition (⌧ Rue du

Mont-Blanc 17 ☎ 022 731 6544). Come Prima has leather handbags as well all sorts of other gifts, while Swiss Tradition sells quality Swiss craftwork – cuckoo clocks, wood carvings etc.

Lausanne

Lausanne's old centre has the best shopping. Bucherer has a shop at Place St Francois 5 (☎ 021 320 6354) and other major names are also represented. Of the Swiss craft outlets the very best is Langenthal at Rue de Bourg 8 (☎ 021 323 4402), which has a range of authentic embroidered linen.

Luzern

The old centre of Luzern is also the place to go. Bucherer and Gubelin both have watch/jewellery shops in the area. Luzern is also very good for linen. Be sure to check as some shops sell Far East made items. To be sure it is probably best to stick to the better known shops such as Sturzenegger (⊠ Schwanenplatz 7 ☎ 041 410 1958) and Neff (⊠ Löwenstrasse 10 ☎ 041 410 1965). For department stores, head for Manor (⊠ Weggisgasse 5 ☎ 041 419 7699) or EPA (⊠ Rössligasse 20 ☎ 041 410 1977).

Lugano

The pedestrianised old centre of Lugano is good, though the modern shopping complex in Quartiere Maghetti offers more choice in a small area. The best departmental store is Innovazione in Piazza Dante (☎ 091 912 7171). For a superb range of handicrafts

go to Bottega dell'Artigiano (⊠ Via Canova 18 ☎ 091 922 8140), which is the outlet for the Ticino Craftsman Co-operative.

Zürich

Zürich, as might be imagined, has the greatest range, much of it concentrated in Bahnhofstrasse where there are big department stores and many boutiques. The biggest departmental stores are Grieder les Boutiques (often claimed as the best in the country) at Bahnhofstrasse 30 (☎ 01 211 3360), which includes sections for such names as Dior and Valentino, and Jelmoli (⊠ Bahnhofstrasse 69 ☎ 01 220 4411). As well as the options in Grieder, the city has outlets of all the major international companies. For designer goods at cheaper prices go to Milano-Zürich (⊠ Usteristrasse 23 ☎ 01 212 0068), which is an outlet for famous names such as Moschino and Cerruti, but at reduced rates. For local fashion, try Sormustin (⊠ Ankerstrasse 41 ☎ 01 240 2606). For linen Spitzenhaus (Börsenstrasse 30 ☎ 01 211 5576) and Sturzenegger (⊠ Bahnhofstrasse 48 ☎ 01 211 2820) should be visited, each selling the genuine article. Leder-Locher at Bahnhofstrasse 91 (☎ 01 211 7082) and Münsterhof 18/19 (☎ 01 211 1864) are best for leather, while for handcrafted gifts and souvenirs go to Meister Silber (⊠ Bahnhofstrasse 28A ☎ 01 221 2730).

The Swiss Army Knife

World-renowned, the red knife with the white cross began life in the late 19th century as an accessory for Swiss soldiers, just as the name says. It is now carried by almost all outdoor enthusiasts and sportsmen as a way of keeping misery at bay with its multi-function blades. As more have been added, so the knife has become larger, some now seeming ludicrously large and unwieldy because of the addition of screwdrivers, bottle and can openers, scissors, piercers, borers, files, things for getting boy scouts out of horses' hoofs and not forgetting knives. If you are intending to buy, the best makes are Victorinox and Wenger.

Activities &
Entertainment

For Children
With cable cars, lake steamers, trains and the numerous sporting opportunities there is little chance children will be bored. Just in case, there are specifically children-orientated sites in all cities, and most towns. These include play areas, swimming pools, theme parks and toy museums. One of the best sites is the Swissminiatur at Melide on Lake Lugano where the entire country (more or less) has been replicated in miniature, complete with model trains and cable cars.

Activities and entertainment opportunities in Switzerland are boundless. Whatever the season you will encounter festivals and concerts during the day and evening. In the principal cities and resorts there is always something happening after the day's sport, including nightclubs and discos.

Hiking
In the mountain areas walks of any length can be made along well-marked paths with frequent signs giving the time, rather than the distance, to the next destination. Using local transport, particularly the famous post-buses, linear walks can be devised to supplement the circular walks possible from most towns and villages.

Mountain sports
Climbing is also popular, the Swiss guide system allowing relative newcomers to enjoy the sport and more experienced climbers to tackle the impressive higher peaks. The Matterhorn is climbed by guided parties virtually all fine summer days.
Few places offer a more spectacular backdrop for hang-gliding and paragliding than the Swiss Alps, and skiing and snow-boarding are, of course, one of the main activities sought by visitors to Switzerland.

Watersports
Those looking for excitement of a different kind could try rafting, canoeing or canyoning in the occasionally fast flowing rivers. The Swiss lakes are also excellent for sailing and windsurfing, particularly for beginners as the winds tend to be very dependable. Opportunites for swimming are found at all altitudes. Lidos have been established by lakes and rivers, and there are numerous indoor and outdoor pools.

Festivals
There are a great number of local festivals in Switzerland, these taking place throughout the year. Ask at the local Tourist Information Office for details. As well as the local festivals there are a number of important international events. Montreux is home to the Television Festival in early May and also to one of Europe's premier jazz festivals in July. Luzern is home to an international music festival in the late summer.

Nightlife
The nightlife is as good in Switzerland as any other European country, particularly in the larger towns. In Zürich the Kaufleten (✉ Pelikenstrasse 18 ☎ 01 225 3300) has maintained its reputation as one of the best night spots in town, smoothly altering its music to align with modern young taste. In Bern Temple (✉ Aarbergstrasse 61 ☎ 031)311 5041) is the current favourite with the younger crowd. In Genève the place to be and to be seen to be is Arthur's Club (Centre ICC, 20 Route de Prés-Bois ☎ 022 791 7700), while in Luzern it is The Loft (✉ Haldenstrasse 2 ☎ 041 410 9244).

Acknowledgements

The Automobile Association would like to thank the following photographers, libraries and agencies for their assistance in the preparation of this book.

Alpen Region Tourism F/C e22b; 38c; 43b; Bern Tourism 36c; Berner Oberland Tourism 34; Brig Tourism 84c; Brunnen Tourism F/C b, f, 21c, 50; Copyright Diablarets Tourisme 87l; Davos Tourism 94, 95, 96t, 96b, 97, 100l, 101, 102t, 103, 104t, 105, 106t, 107t, 107b, 108, 109t, 110l, 111t, 111b, 112; Engelberg-Titlus Tourismus AG 21tl, 52; Geneva Tourism 62, 63; Interlaken Tourism 40b, 41c; Kunstmuseum, Basel 30, 31; Lausanne Tourism (© Stephen Engler) 64; Leventina Tourism 18c, 70c; Lugano Tourisme 75b; Maggiore Tourisme 70b, 72r, 74; MRI Bankers Guide to Foreign Currency 9; Nyon Region Tourisme 67; Office de Tourisme du Canton de Vaud F/C a; Picture Tourist Office Pontresina 18b, 98; Rigi Tourism 54/55, 55c, 104b; Saas-Fee Tourism 80, 81, 82t, 83t, 84t, 86t, 87r, 88l, 89, 90t, 90b, 91t, 91c, 92t, 93; Tourism Board St. Moritz 5, 14t, 15t, 15b, 16t, 17t, 18t, 19r, 20t, 21tr, 22t, 24t, 24c, 25t, 26, 27, 99l, 109b; Villars Tourism (Studio Patrick Jantet Villars) 92c; Wengen Tourism 47c; World Trade Organisation 17b; Zuos Tourism 102/103; Zurich Tourismus F/C d, 7t, 14b, 20b, 21b, 23b, 28, 29, 32, 33

The remaining images are held in the Association's own library (**AA WORLD TRAVEL LIBRARY**) with contributions from Adrian Baker F/C g, back cover, 1, 2, 6b, 7b, 42, 46b, 73b, 76/77, 86b, 100b; and Steve Day F/C c, background image, 6t, 19l, 35, 36t, 37, 38t, 39, 40t, 41t, 43t, 44t, 44r, 45t, 45b, 46t, 47t, 48, 49, 51t, 51b, 53, 54, 55t, 55t, 56, 57, 58, 58/59, 59, 60, 61, 54t, 65b, 66, 68, 69, 70t, 71t, 71c, 72l, 73t, 75t, 76, 77, 78t, 78b, 79l, 79r, 82b, 85, 88, 88/89, 109c, 109b, 110r

Contributors
Compiled from material commissioned by AA Publishing
Compiled and edited by Jackie Staddon and Hilary Weston
Additional original text by Richard Sale

Dear Essential Traveller

**Your comments, opinions and recommendations are very
important to us. So please help us to improve our travel
guides by taking a few minutes to complete this simple
questionnaire.**

*You do not need a stamp (unless posted outside the UK). If you do not want to cut this page
from your guide, then photocopy it or write your answers on a plain sheet of paper.*

Send to: **The Editor, AA World Travel Guides,
FREEPOST SCE 4598, Basingstoke RG21 4GY.**

Your recommendations…

We always encourage readers' recommendations for restaurants, nightlife
or shopping – if your recommendation is used in the next edition of the
guide, we will send you a *FREE* AA *Essential* **Guide** of your choice.
Please state below the establishment name, location and your reasons
for recommending it.

_____

_____

_____

_____

Please send me **AA *Essential*** _____
(*see list of titles inside the front cover*)

About this guide…

Which title did you buy?
AA *Essential* _____
Where did you buy it? _____
When? m m / y y

Why did you choose an AA *Essential* Guide? _____

_____

_____

_____

_____

Did this guide meet your expectations?
Exceeded ☐   Met all ☐   Met most ☐   Fell below ☐
Please give your reasons _____

_____

_____

_____

continued on next page…

Were there any aspects of this guide that you particularly liked? _____

_____

_____

_____

Is there anything we could have done better? _____

_____

_____

_____

_____

About you...

Name (*Mr/Mrs/Ms*) _____

    Address _____

_____

_____ Postcode _____

    Daytime tel nos _____

Which age group are you in?

  Under 25 ☐ 25–34 ☐ 35–44 ☐ 45–54 ☐ 55–64 ☐ 65+ ☐

How many trips do you make a year?

  Less than one ☐ One ☐ Two ☐ Three or more ☐

Are you an AA member? Yes ☐ No ☐

About your trip...

When did you book? m m / y y   When did you travel? m m / y y

How long did you stay? _____

Was it for business or leisure? _____

Did you buy any other travel guides for your trip?

  If yes, which ones? _____

_____

Thank you for taking the time to complete this questionnaire. Please send
it to us as soon as possible, and remember, you do not need a stamp
(*unless posted outside the UK*).

Happy Holidays!